CONTENTS

Central Corfu → p. 80

Trips & Tours → p. 94

Road atlas → p. 124

DID YOU KNOW?
Timeline → p. 12
Corfu becomes multicultural
→ p. 22
Specialities → p. 26
Esoteric centres → p. 55
The fish cult → p. 75
Little oranges → p. 92
Weather in Corfu → p. 113
Books & Films → p. 114
Currency converter → p. 116
Budgeting → p. 117

MAPS IN THE GUIDEBOOK
(126 A1) Page numbers
and coordinates refer to
the road atlas
(0) Site/address located off
the map coordinates are also
given for places that are not
marked on the road atlas
(U A1) Refers to the map
inside the back cover

**INSIDE BACK COVER:
PULL-OUT MAP →**

PULL-OUT MAP 🔲
(🔲 A1) Refers to the
removable pull-out map
(🔲 a1) Refers to the map
on the back of the
pull-out map

The best MARCO POLO Insider Tips

Our top 15 Insider Tips

INSIDER TIP **Fresh and tasty**

The Bellissimo Taverna is hidden away just a few yards off the Old Town's main shopping street. Three generations provide a friendly service and new delicacies every day → **p. 43**

INSIDER TIP **Royal bay**

Only a few visitors to Corfu know about the small bay in Mon Repos Park where royalty used to bathe → **p. 45**

INSIDER TIP **Up high**

Only a tiny sign in front of the Hotel Cavalieri draws attention to its roof garden with its enticing sundaes and cocktails high above the Old Town (photo right) → **p. 46**

INSIDER TIP **A room with a view**

The Hotel Konstantinoúpolis, built in 1861, hardly stands out from the other buildings on the Old Harbour. But, you have a view all the way to Albania from its windows and balconies → **p. 46**

INSIDER TIP **Relax in a lemon grove**

The Lemon Garden in Acharávi is the place to sit – central, but completely secluded – and enjoy a drink, cake or fine food surrounded by citrus trees → **p. 51**

INSIDER TIP **Cheap and cheerful**

The simple Hotel Róda Inn on the north coast provides superb value for money and the atmosphere is just great → **p. 52**

INSIDER TIP **Lobster without frills**

The Gregóris Taverna is located off the beaten track above the usually deserted Astrakéri Beach and serves lobsters at reasonable prices, prepared just the way the fishermen themselves like them → **p. 53**

INSIDER TIP **Buddha on Corfu**

The island's most unusual church can be found on the outskirts of Nímfes – it looks like a Buddhist stupa → **p. 53**

MARCO ⊕ POLO

Travel with **Insider Tips**

CORFU

SERBIA
MNE KSV BUL.
MAC.
Bari ALBANIA
ITALY TURKEY
Igoumenitsa
Corfu
Athens
Sicily
(I)
MALTA GREECE
Crete
Mediterranean Sea
EGYPT

SYMBOLS

INSIDER TIP	Insider Tip
★	Highlight
●●●●	Best of …
☆	Scenic view

🌿 Responsible travel: for eco-
logical or fair trade aspects

(*) Telephone numbers that
are not toll-free

**PRICE CATEGORIES
HOTELS**

Expensive   over 80 euros

Moderate   50–80 euros

Budget   under 50 euros

Price for a double room,
without breakfast,
in the high season

**PRICE CATEGORIES
RESTAURANTS**

Expensive   over 16 euros

Moderate   12–16 euros

Budget   under 12 euros

Prices for a meat dish with
potatoes, a Greek salad and
half a bottle of house wine

On the cover: Picture perfect panorama: Cape Drástis p. 56 | Time stands still in Paleó Perítha p. 53

INSIDER TIP Cruise the coast

A small motorboat is moored at the end of the track to Cape Drástis and its skipper takes those who make their way here on short trips along the rocky coast → **p. 54**

INSIDER TIP Farm holidays

Anna takes loving care of the Little Farmhouse's 4000 olive trees. If you rent her old stone house, you'll learn everything about olive cultivation and can enjoy the organic vegetables from her garden → **p. 58**

INSIDER TIP Magnificent garden

You will feel like you are in paradise if you stay in the Pension Skála in Paramónas with its wonderfully laid out gardens → **p. 75**

INSIDER TIP A stroll in a park with temples

A stroll under 150-year-old shady trees with a view of the Ionian Sea takes you past the remains of two ancient temples → **p. 94**

INSIDER TIP Hike across the island

You can hike across the island on the 200 km (125 mi) long Corfu Trail. You should be something of a trailblazer; the paths are not perfectly marked but there is always a village in sight on Corfu → **p. 102**

INSIDER TIP Riding for everyone

Sally-Ann Lewis used to be a cowgirl in Wyoming. Since 1992, she has been taking riders of all levels on two-hour trails through Corfu's olive groves and vineyards. Trailraiders' stables are near the village of Áno Korakiána → **p. 102**

INSIDER TIP Keep fit

The Corfu Mountainbike Shop in Dassiá offers everything a biker needs. The services offered by the MTB pros range from rentals to guided day tours and a complete Fly-&-Bike programme → **p. 102**

BEST OF ...

GREAT PLACES FOR FREE
Discover new places and save money

● **Free culture**
Rock festivals, jazz concerts, operas and concerts with traditional Corfiot orchestras – and all free of charge or for a token 1 cent fee! On no less than 30 evenings between early June and mid August the annual International Festival of Corfu bans boredom from the island → p. 109

● **Captivating views**
Onassis would certainly have paid a fortune for such a view. The panoramic view from the Kanóni lookout point near the town towards Mouse Island and the monastery island of Vlachérna makes millionaires envious and captivates painters and artists. Some action comes into the picture when jets full of holiday-makers swoop down at eye-level before landing (photo, below) → p. 38 and 107

● **Graffiti, graffiti everywhere**
Once an insider tip for hippies, now a unique open-air museum for lovers of modern street art. More than a mile of concrete wall in the mountain village of Pélekas has been painted by international graffiti artists – and more works are welcome → p. 89

● **From pool to pool**
How about a bit of pool-hopping? You can often swim in the pools at many smaller hotels even if you are not a guest – as long as you buy a drink at the bar. A change of scenery is always good → p. 73

● **Open invitation to night-owls**
Nightlife in Corfu Town is not nearly as expensive as you might think. Very few of the venues in the popular clubbing district around the ferry terminal charge entry fees. Get ready to party the night away → p. 64

● **A table with a view – and a sunbed**
If you choose to have lunch in the beautifully situated Panórama taverna in Petríti you can indulge in a further luxury free of charge after an excellent meal – namely the use of sunbeds on the beach nearby → p. 79

◯◉◉◉◉ Dots in guidebook refer to 'Best of ...' tips

ONLY IN CORFU
Unique experiences

● *Watch out – keep your head down!*
The Corfiots celebrate Easter in their own very special way. On Easter Saturday hundreds of clay water jugs are thrown out of windows and from balconies onto the streets in the Old Town. Thousands watch this spectacle that follows the magnificent Easter procession → p. 109

● *Little oranges are big business*
The bitter fruit of the cumquat tree has become a new trademark of the island. Try them yourself! Liqueurs, jams, sweets and many other goodies can be found in the shop run by the Vassilákis family in the town or its sales rooms at Achíllion (photo) → p. 29, 45 and 92

● *A lifetime working with olive wood*
Olive trees provide fruit and oil as well as a unique kind of wood that demands great skill from carvers. For decades Thomás has been one of the best and has devoted himself to this craft in his 'Atelier by Tom' in the Old Town → p. 44

● *Moments of contemplation*
Linger for a while in Corfu's most important church Ágios Spirídonas and experience the locals' religious tradition first hand. There is a continuous stream of Corfiots who kiss the icons, pay homage to the relics of the patron saint of the island and kneel in prayer, as many feel this is the place – between paintings, icons and the silver sarcophagus of St. Spirídon – where heaven and earth meet → p. 39

● *Fish in the Garden of Eden*
Corfiots love lush gardens and a fish soup called *bourdétto* made with scorpion fish. In Alonáki Taverna near Chalikúnas you can enjoy the best of both – a version of the traditional dish made to a particularly tasty recipe, served in beautiful surroundings → p. 70

● *In perfect harmony*
Dance like Zorba the Greek! Thanks to the blockbuster film of the same name, the *sirtáki* has become synonymous with Greek dancing. You can delight in watching professional dancers perform on the terrace at the *Golden Beach* bar and actually give it a try yourself! → p. 86

ONLY IN

BEST OF ...

● *Look the monster in the eye*
A visit to the *Archaeological Museum* will show just how gifted Corfu's sculptors were 2600 years ago. The terrifyingly grotesque face of the Gorgo is a real masterpiece (photo) → p. 35

● *Shopping under the arcades*
The arcades of the main shopping streets in the Old Town, especially Odós N. Theotóki, protect shoppers from the scorching heat and downpours → p. 44

● *Jewellery with a personal touch*
Shells that you find while walking along a beach can be transformed into lovely pieces of jewellery. Corfu's natural jewels can be cast in gold, silver or bronze at the Ílios Centre in Ágios Geórgios Pagón → p. 56

● *Just go under*
If you really want to get the better of the rain, just go under water. On board the Calypso Star you can look through the large window in the hull at the undersea world → p. 42 and 106

● *Olive-oil soap*
Take a trip 150 years back in time in the Patoúnis soap factory. A warm welcome awaits visitors to the production facilities and storerooms where you can take all the pictures you want and buy at reasonable prices. Saturday is the best day to visit – that is when the soap is boiled → p. 44

● *Lean back and enjoy a rainy day*
There's no such thing as a black cloud in the Ey Lounge. It's even a favourite place for friends to meet for breakfast; at lunchtime you can soak up the local atmosphere as it fills with the business crowd and in the evenings the lounge launches you straight into that perfect night out clubbing! → p. 43

RAIN

RELAX AND CHILL OUT
Take it easy and spoil yourself

● *Let yourself be pampered*
The spa area in the St. George's Bay Country Club & Spa is one of the newest on the island. It is designed like a Corfiot village with its unique country-house architecture → **p. 52**

● *A spot of cricket*
Stop by for a few overs and spend a relaxing Sunday afternoon in the *Café on the Esplanade* in Kérkyra sipping a cocktail while watching the locals bat and bowl on the well-kept pitch – just like being at home → **p. 55**

● *Take the boat to Páxos*
Sail away from the mainland, let the sea breeze blow in your face and leave the steering to someone else. Take a relaxing boat trip to Corfu's sister island, Páxos (photo, below). Ships depart for the little isle from Kérkyra, Messongi-Moraítika and Kávos → **p. 98**

● *Down on the farm*
If you want to be far from the madding crowd then you'll enjoy your stay with Anna Polychroniádou. The organic farmer's holiday let is simply called 'Little Farmhouse' where you can watch the donkeys and collect your eggs for breakfast from the chicken coop → **p. 58**

● *Zen as a way of life*
You'll feel like you are in a Buddhist Zen monastery in the Corfu Meditation House. Day guests are also welcome to come and meditate in Zen-Do and its garden → **p. 55**

● *Awash with orchids*
The romantically inclined will love the British Cemetery. In spring and autumn, this fairy-tale oasis is a mass of wild orchids flowering among the gravestones → **p. 37**

INTRODUCTION

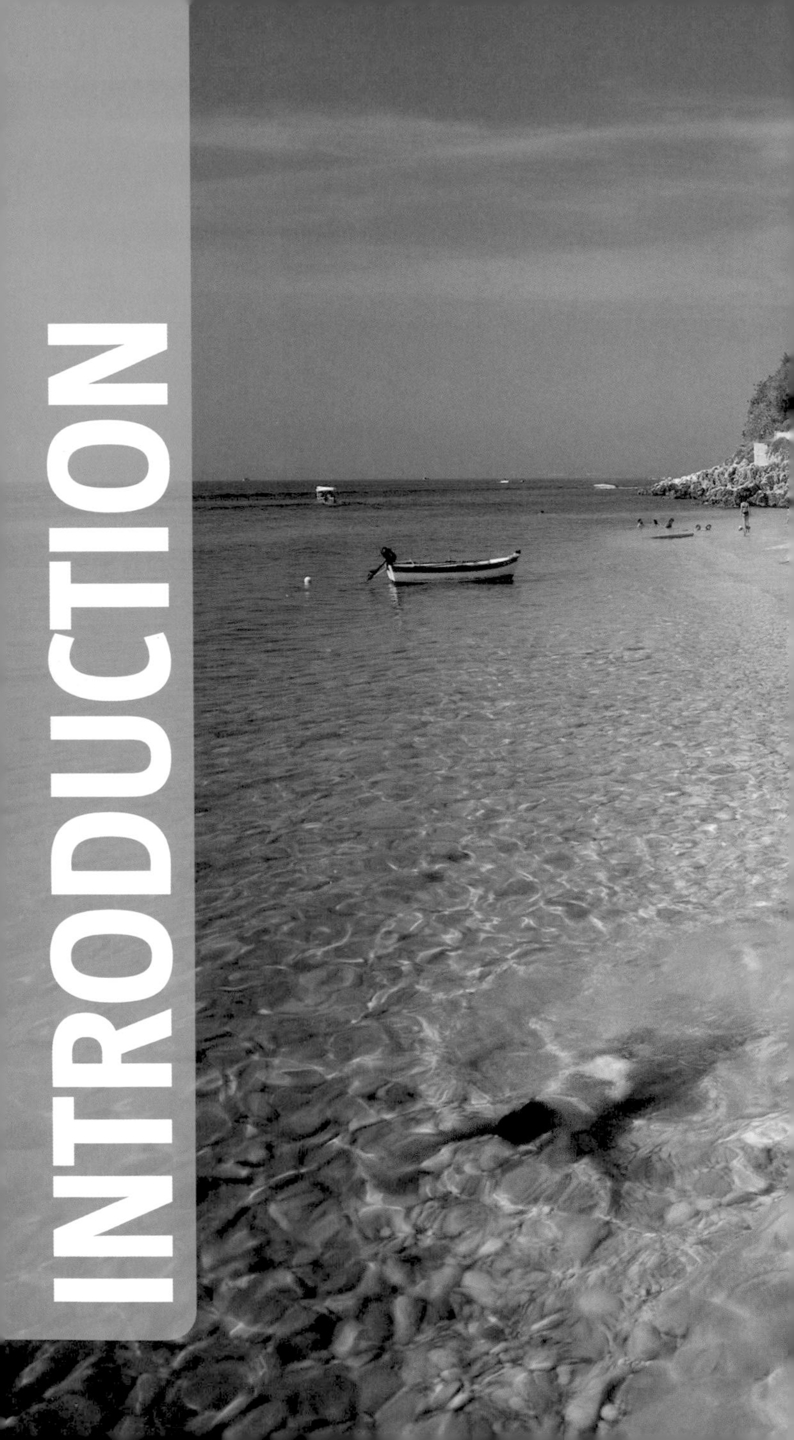

DISCOVER CORFU!

The plane starts its descent where the Adriatic merges into the Ionian Sea. The first small Greek islands welcome you from below. Then Corfu rises up out of the sea. In the north, the narrow sandy beaches are bordered by an impressive, steep coastline; further south, wide bays are fringed with broad sandy beaches. The island (population 112,000 inhabitants) is the most northerly and, with its 611 sq km (236 sq mi), the second largest in the Ionian Sea.

The plane descends even lower, glides over a dense carpet of olive groves interspersed with the sharp tops of cypresses. Centuries-old villages dream below, hidden away on the hillsides, mountain slopes and in the small valleys. We fly on over the island's

Photo: Kalamáki Beach

capital where we get a clear view of the harbour and the two Venetian castles that form the boundary of the Old Town. The high mountains on the Greek and Albanian mainland soar up on the other side of the strait. A radio beacon at Lefkími lets the pilot know it is time to turn and the final descent begins. He soon sinks below the ridges of the green hills on the coast and appears to almost brush the villages along the shoreline. It looks like the plane is going to land on the water but it sets down accurately on the runway that was built in a lagoon.

The Corfu experience begins! Kérkyra – the name the Greeks use for the town and the whole island – is just a short walk from the airport. The path leads us along the promenade towards the Old Fortress, one of the five Venetian castles on the island. The green expanse of the Esplanade opens out in front of its entrance. The British gave free rein to their eccentricity: they placed a water tank in the shape of an ancient temple at one end and an imposing palace for their island administrator at the other. There is a statue of one of them – wearing a Roman toga – in front of it.

Pavement cafés under shady arcades

The French, who controlled the island for a short time before the British, were more sensible: they left a row of pavement cafés under the shady arcades behind them. That is where the old Corfiots like to sip their Greek coffee, while the younger ones prefer iced coffee. This is a real hotspot in the early evening when the Corfiots celebrate their traditional *volta* – promenading back and forth in front of the cafés to see and be seen. There is more activity on the broad, marble-paved streets between the

734 BC
With the founding of a colony by the Greek city of Corinth, Corfu becomes part of the world of classical Greece

229 BC
Corfu is the first Greek town to submit to the rule of the up-and-coming world power Rome

395–1204 AD
East-Roman Byzantine period; Corfu ruled from Constantinople

1386
The Venetians take over Corfu that develops into one of its most important possessions in the Mediterranean and resists two Turkish conquest campaigns in the 16th century

Empress 'Sisi' built it as a holiday home, Kaiser Wilhelm II loved it: Villa Achíllion

Esplanade and Old Harbour with all their enticing shops under the arcades. There are many more shops in the former Jewish area in the Old Town, Evraiki, while the largest district Cambiéllo is entirely residential.

Kérkyra is a perfect year-round destination for a city trip. However, there are hardly any other cultural attractions anywhere else on the island. On the one hand, there has been little excavation activity because the ancient settlements are now the sites of modern housing and, on the other, its position on the periphery of ancient Greece made it less important.

Only when the Venetians took over control of the island in 1386 did Corfu gain in status. The new rulers used it principally as a provider of olive oil, which was used for lighting at that time, and did all they could to promote the cultivation of olive trees.

1453
The Byzantine Empire collapses; the Turks control all of Greece – with the exception of the Ionian Islands

1797–1864
Napoleon occupies the Ionian Islands that subsequently gain independence under Russian and Turkish protection. In 1807, French again; 1809, British; and, after 1815, an independent republic under the protection of Great Britain

1864
The Ionian Islands become part of free Greece

1941–1944
Italian and German occupation

The Corfiots have the Venetians to thank for never coming under Turkish dominance. There is absolutely no Turkish or oriental influence on Corfu. That also makes the island quite different: there are no mosques as there are elsewhere in Greece. Corfiot folk music lacks the oriental touch of the Aegean and the Ionian Islands – with Corfu as the main one – as it also followed its own individual artistic path.

The summer holidaymakers are mainly interested in the beaches. The island is surrounded by them and there is such a great variety that everybody can find that perfect dream beach. Those on the east coast facing the mainland, where most of the large seaside hotels are located, are mostly of shingles or smooth pebbles, often several hundred metres long and always fairly narrow. Many of the hotels directly on the beach offset this by providing lush, green lawns around the pool, tavernas place deck-chairs in their flowery gardens and hang hammocks between the trees. Wooden jetties jut out into the protected bays of the straits. This is where the sun worshipers lie, before climbing down ladders into the water. Some are used as water-sport centres. The east coast is perfect for waterskiing, paragliding and for paddle boats – however, surfers will be rather disappointed. This area, with its gently sloping beaches, is ideal for families with children. The bathing shoes that can be bought in any supermarket increase the pleasure even more.

> **The west coast has a great variety of beaches**

The north coast is better suited for those who like long, wide beaches. The tavernas and lounge bars make a stopover on long strolls along the beach even more enjoyable. It is especially worth visiting them at sunset when the fiery ball sinks into the sea somewhere between the last Greek island of Othoní and the Albanian mainland.

Corfu's west coast facing the open sea offers the greatest variety of beaches. They begin at Cape Drástis in the far northwest where the brave climb into the water from white rocks and, if the sea is completely calm, swim out along the white sandstone cliffs. Near Peruládes, steps lead down from the steep coast to the long, narrow sandy beach stretching under the cliffs. The golden crescents of sand in the bays of Ágios Stéfanos and Ágios Geórgios Pagón are miles long while most of the 20+ beaches on the fragmented Paleokastritsa Bay are hidden away and can only be reached by boat.

1967–1974
Military dictatorship followed by emergence of democracy

2002
The euro replaces the drachma as the national currency

2004
The Olympic Games are held in Athens

2010
Greece can only be saved from national bankruptcy through financial aid from the European Union and the International Monetary Fund. Drastic tax increases, pension and salary cuts, as well as an increase in the age of retirement, are intended to reduce the national debt

Kérkyra's squares: Laid-back meeting places with a not an historical background

Some large hotels have opened on the few beaches in the middle of the west coast: in Glifáda, Pélekas and Ágios Górdis. It then becomes more secluded. The beach at the northern spit between the sea and Lake Chalikúnas is almost completely deserted and the few bathers to the southwest of the lake lose themselves in the expansive, Sahara-like dunes of Ágios Geórgios Argirádon. In the extreme south, a noisy counterpoint is provided by Kávos with its narrow strips of sand where there is an all-day party and plenty of close contact on the beach.

No matter how attractive the beaches are: the interior of the island is just as beautiful and varied. Many narrow, rollercoaster-like paths lead uphill and down dale to fresh lookout points. If you leave the beaches, you will come across many small villages

Where Greek hospitality is still very much alive

that are hardly ever visited by tourists and where you can still experience traditional Greek hospitality. One of the last nuns in the convent near Lefkími might even invite you to a cup of Greek coffee that they – like many other Corfiots – perk up with a shot of ouzo. When you visit a church, the sacristan will often give you a piece of blessed bread without being asked; in a fish tavern in Búkari, you can pick your own dessert from the fruit trees in the garden. These are gestures of human warmth that the Corfiots also appreciate receiving from their visitors. In this way, your holiday will be full of happy memories.

WHAT'S HOT

1 Hellas Sirtáki

Traditional dancing boom For a long time, sirtáki was only danced by the locals at traditional festivities. Now, arms are spread and off they go on other occasions. On several evenings of the week there is live music in the *Luna d'argento* where professional dancers show you the right steps *(Ano Korakiana, www.lunacorfu.com)*. The *Alios* group is one of the local star acts and they also give lessons *(www.alios-corfu.com)*. Classical sirtáki is performed on the terrace of the ● Golden Beach Bar. After the experts, the audience joins in *(on Moraítika Beach, www.goldenbeach.com)*. The film 'Zorba the Greek' made the dance world famous – and Jane Fonda and Anthony Quinn, who danced it in Tripa, true film stars *(on the village square in Kinopiástes, www.tripas.gr)*.

Past and present

● ***Corfu swings the bat*** In the 19th century, the British brought cricket to Corfu. After they left, interest died down but there has been a revival in recent years. The young Corfiots now increasingly pick up the bat and ball. On Sunday afternoons, bats are swung on the neatly trimmed grass pitch in Kérkyra – you can watch the pros and amateurs in comfort from the *Café on the Esplanade*. Enthusiastic players will explain the rules to you over a chat in the shade. Cricket tournaments do not take place in the sweltering summer months. There was even a *Cricket Festival (http://festival.cricket.gr)* on the island in 2010. The sporting event is planned to be held annually and is organised by the *Hellenic Cricket Foundation* that also has its headquarters on Corfu *(www.cricket.gr)*.

Fresh and organic

Self-sufficient Corfu has now recognised that home-made tastes best. The *Etrusco Restaurant* uses fresh products from its own garden as much as possible. In 2010, the renowned chef Ettore Botrini laid out his garden and planted the ingredients for his Etrusco Salad together with fresh herbs and flowers, as well as for dishes with intriguing names like 'lamb with sweet garlic and cumquats'. Don't miss the home-made sausages and salami *(Káto Korakiána, www.etrusco.gr, photo).* Kostas and Agathi Vlassi also use products from their own farm. Fresh eggs and bread baked in a wood-fired oven are served at breakfast in their *Hotel Restaurant Bioporos* and there are authentic dishes cooked using traditional recipes for lunch and dinner. All of the products from their 10-acre farm are organic *(near Vrakaniotika, www.bioporos.gr).*

New sensations

Walking on water Waterskiing is old hat. The sporty no longer need a boat to pull them across the water on skis. The Aqua Striders invented by Niko Gatsios make this possible. With these special, air-filled skis, the adventurous can glide across the water at speeds of between 5 and 10 km/h – with no help at all from an outboard motor. Poles similar to those used for skiing with buoys at the end, or simple paddles, help you keep your balance. You can try out this sports innovation which caused a sensation at the *International Exhibition of Inventions*, at the *Corfu Ski Club* at the *Hotel Daphnila Bay Thalasso (Dassiá)* and at *Dassiá Beach.*

IN A NUTSHELL

AGÍA, ÁGIOS, ÁGII

You will come across the three little words *agía, ágios* and *ágii* all over the island. They form part of the names of villages and churches, as well as fishing boats and ferries. *Agía* is a female saint, *ágios* a male saint and *ágii* the plural form. If this is preceded by *moní* (monastery), the genitive form is used (*ágias, ágiou* and *ágion*). The Mother of God is worthy of a special title; she is the *Panagía* – the 'all holy'.

BUILDING BOOM

One of the disconcerting characteristics of Corfu are the many unfinished buildings. There are two main reasons for this: the Greeks have long mistrusted their banks and the stability of their currency – not just since the financial crisis – and therefore invest their savings in property. However, there is often not enough cash to finish building in one go and work is only carried out as long as the money lasts. In addition, many Greeks still feel obliged to at least give their children a flat when they marry. Plans are made when the children are still young, or even before their birth – that way, there is enough time to save for extensions to the family home.

BYZANTIUM

Historians usually refer to the Byzantine era when talking about

Icons, kiosks and olive groves –
Useful information for your holiday
on Corfu

Greece in the Middle Ages. It almost exactly coincides with the medieval period and began with Emperor Justinian in the 6th century and ended with the Turkish conquest of Constantinople in 1453. Constantinople – today's Istanbul – was the capital of the empire that once spread from the Straits of Gibraltar to well into the Middle East and North Africa. Corfu was also part of it until the beginning of the 13th century.

DROPPING OUT OR ADOPTING A NEW LIFESTYLE

After a holiday on Corfu, many people dream of settling permanently on the island. Currently, around 900 Brits live here and many other nationalities. As long as the foreigners spend money and don't try to open up a shop or pub, they are welcomed by the Corfiots. If they try to compete with the locals, they can count on regular official inspections and even damage to their property. Only those who are really innovative and provide something that is completely new have a chance of being accepted.

FAUNA

Dogs and cats are the animals you will most often encounter on Corfu. Wild mammals have become rare. You are more likely to see dead foxes, martens, hedgehogs and weasels on the roadside there are several non-poisonous ones including the Montpelier snake and various whip snakes. There are many tortoises and hardly any scorpions. In the early summer glow-worms cast their light. Overfishing has depleted the sea but you might spot some dolphins if you are lucky.

FLAGS

A second flag is often hoisted in front of churches along with the white-and-blue Greek national flag. This is the offi-

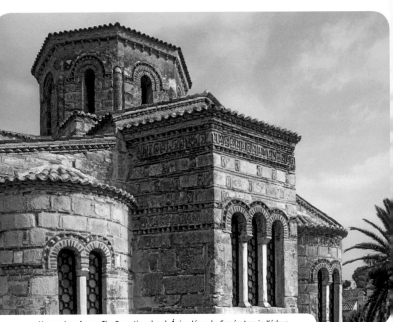
Harmonious forms: The Byzantine church Ágios Jáson ke Sossípatros in Kérkyra

than live ones. The bird world is more varied with orioles, hoopoes, jays, small owls, swallows and swifts. Buzzards and falcons are sometimes spotted in secluded mountain regions and herons can be found on the low-lying coasts.

The only poisonous snake you might come across on a hike is the sand adder, but

cial flag of the Greek Orthodox Church and shows the black, Byzantine double-eagle on a yellow background.

HOLIDAYS

The Greek summer holidays last from the middle of June to mid-September. August is the main holiday month and hardly any Greeks stay at home between 1 and 20 August. They almost all flock to the seashore, a lot of them to the islands. That is also when many Italians spend their holidays here and it is difficult to find accommodation during this period without booking in advance.

CONS

Icons are panel paintings of the Orthodox Church showing saints and Biblical scenes. They can be found in all houses of worship as well as in cars, buses, shops, restaurants and homes. In addition to the classical icons that are common all over the former Byzantine region, those paintings influenced by Italian art which resemble western religious painting are also called icons and can be found in many of Corfu's churches and museums. Believers honour them as they do any other icon although they lack the criteria for being considered genuine icons (such as an inscription and the lack of a central perspective).

Even today, a classical icon painter has very little freedom and has to observe ancient rules. Imagination and artistic creativity are not asked for – only his talents as a craftsman. This results in many icons resembling each other regardless of when they were painted.

All icons are regarded as 'gates to heaven'. They bring the presence of a saint into the home. His eyes, which almost always look straight at the observer, create the access that makes it possible for the spirit of the believer to unite with that of the depicted. That is why icons are treated with such respect. They are kissed and decorated with all sorts of different precious metals, fitted with curtains or draped in valuable materials, incorporated in decorative timepieces and carried in processions around the church, through the village, across fields and through olive groves.

KAMÁKIA

Women travelling alone will not stay that way for long on Corfu. The *kamákia* (literally: 'harpoons') take care of that. They are always fashionably dressed with a gold chain on their half-bared chest and can start up a conversation in almost any language. Many of them work as waiters or souvenir dealers. However, in their defence, it must be said that some *kamáki* have ended up marrying one of their holiday acquaintances.

KIOSKS

Kiosks – in Greek, the singular noun *períptero* is used – can be found on every square in Kérkyra as well as in the villages and at many major crossroads. They are usually open from early in the morning to late at night and offer everything you need in a hurry or forget to buy when the shops were open: newspapers, cigarettes, sweets, batteries and telephone cards, toothbrushes and combs, single aspirin tablets, condoms and much more.

KOMBOLÓI

Many Greeks – and that includes the Corfiots – always have a *kombolói*, a string of beads similar to a rosary, with them. It has no religious significance but is merely seen as a way of passing the time or as a lucky charm. The Greeks probably adopted it from the Islamic prayer beads.

LOTTERY TICKET SELLERS

Lottery ticket sellers are just as much part of everyday life on Corfu as priests and kiosks. There are two kinds of tickets: scratch cards where you win immediately and tickets for the national lottery whose winning numbers are drawn on Monday evenings. With a bit of luck your numbers may come up and pay for your holiday!

ORGANIC FARMERS AND OLIVE GROVES

There are actually many farmers on Corfu who would like to produce organic goods with better prospects for sales and higher prices – especially for wine and olive oil. However, the hurdles are too high as it is difficult for them to keep the minimum distance from the fields and groves of 'chemical farmers' and there is only one press on the island that processes organically grown olives. At least, extensive insecticide spraying from the air has been stopped so that each farmer can decide on the fertilizers and chemicals he wants to have on his property.

Just how intensive olive cultivation is on Corfu becomes clear in the interior of the island. There, the roads wind through ancient olive groves where the sunlight is filtered through the dense tops of the gnarled trees. Black nets are often spread out on the ground or rolled in the forks of the trees and increase the feeling of being in a dark, enchanted forest. They catch the falling olives between November and March that the farmers and their, usually Albanian, workers collect several times a week and take to the olive presses.

POLITICAL PARTIES

Greece's political landscape is dominated by two major parties: the social-democratic *Pasók* led by Geórgios Papandréou – which won the last election in 2009 – and the conservative *Néa Dimokratia*. Both share the main responsibility for Greece's financial crisis. In order to keep their supporters happy, they created superfluous positions and token jobs in the civil service over decades that will be a burden on the state pension finances for years to come. The smaller parties in the 300-seat Greek parliament are the Communists *KKE*, the left alliance *SYRIZA*, and the right-populist *LAOS*. At the last election *Pasók* received 43.38 percent, the *Néa Dimokratia* 32.83 and the *KKE* 11.95 percent of the votes cast on Corfu.

RELIGION

Almost all Corfiots profess their belief in Greek-Orthodox Christianity. Other

CORFU BECOMES MULTICULTURAL

Globalisation has also not overlooked this small island. Foreigners have always played an important role in determining Corfu's destiny, formerly as rulers with the Corfiots as their helpers. Now life is changing on Corfu. The olive harvest would be impossible without day labourers from Albania and there would be even more fish in the sea without the help of fishermen from the Nile Delta. Many houses would remain unbuilt and many hotel rooms uncleaned without Bulgarian and Romanian muscle power. In former times only Romani people made their way through the villages with their laden-down carts. Today people from Southeast Asia in Korean cars complement this with electronic goods and Africans specialise in illicitly pressed CDs and DVDs. Even the evening entertainment would be less interesting without foreigners. Many hotels and beach bars hire multi-lingual Czechs and Hungarians for their animation programmes.

religions are considered heretic and simply belonging to them blocks the path to heaven. Many holidaymakers remark on the large number of churches and small chapels. The altar is always located in the east behind an iconostasis, a wall of icons. It separates the altar room, which can only be entered by the priests and deacons, from the rest of the church. Believers light candles in front of the icons on the iconostasis and other walls. A constant stream of people come and go throughout the Orthodox service that can last for more than two hours.

You will see Orthodox priests (Greek: *pappádes*, singular *pappás*) wherever you go on Corfu. They wear long, dark robes and a black headdress – often with a braid peeking out from under it. If nature has its way, they are always long-haired and sport a full beard. Before being ordained, priests may marry and often have large families. They augment their state salary with fees for weddings and baptisms. Church taxes are unknown here. Some are farmers or run a taverna or other small business on the side.

The schism, the official church division, in 1054 came as a result of many dogmatic differences. According to the Orthodox Church, the Holy Ghost derives solely from God the Father while the Pope proclaimed that this was equally so with the Father and the Son (Filioque controversy).

WARS

In the past century, Greece suffered more from war than many other European countries: 1904–08, in the war against Bulgaria; 1912–22, the First and Second Balkan Wars, World War I and the anti-Turkish campaign in Asia Minor and, finally, 1940–49, World War II and the Civil War.

During the latter, the Communists and conservatives – supported by the British – confronted each other, even though both had previously fought side by side against the Germans as partisans. There are memorials to the fallen all over Corfu where the names of those who died in all these

Greek-Orthodox priests can be seen all over Corfu

wars are listed; the soldier cemeteries also bear witness to Serbian and French fatalities.

FOOD & DRINK

Tourism has unfortunately made the Greek menu less varied. Many visitors order the same things: moussaká, souvláki, tzaziki and a Greek salad. **More interesting dishes have almost no chance on Corfu – and that is why they are hardly ever available in the summer months.**

Play a role in protecting genuine Greek cooking by trying dishes you don't know. You don't have to go as far as lamb's head *(kefalákia)* or sheep's testicles *(ameléttia)*. Most of the restaurants have menus in several languages and many innkeepers now show photos of their dishes. However, they will usually look different on your plate because the pictures were taken in a studio.

In traditional restaurants, you can see a variety of prepared dishes kept warm, and refrigerated showcases with raw meat waiting to be grilled. It used to be normal to take a look in the pot in many Greek restaurants but this is only rarely permitted nowadays. You always choose your fresh fish from the refrigerator and it is then prepared to your liking.

Greeks love to have a great number of plates, with many different dishes, on the table at a time. They hardly ever go out alone in the evening and a cheerful round of diners, *paréa,* is just as important as the culinary delights. The *paréa* orders many different dishes and they are all placed in the middle of the table. Everybody takes

You can eat gyros at home, so here you should try real Corfiot cuisine – usually late at night and hardly ever alone

what – and as much as – they want. Fish and meat are usually served on large platters and everybody helps themselves. Usually, more is ordered than can be eaten. It is considered a disgrace if everything is eaten up because it shows that, obviously, too little was ordered. All the plates, even the empty ones, are left on the table. The waiters don't take any away so that the *paréa* can see how well they dined.

You can eat at any time. Most of the restaurants that don't only live from tourism are open all day. An English breakfast is often served from 10am and the main meals can be taken any time between 11am and midnight. Only occasionally do some restaurants close between 4 and 6pm. There is usually a *cover charge* of between 20 cents and 3 euros that includes serviettes and bread. You cannot refuse to pay this.

SPECIALITIES

▶ **bakaljáros me skordaljá** – dried hake served with a potato-garlic puree

▶ **bekri mezé** – pork stewed in red wine

▶ **bourdéto** – Corfiot fish or (sometimes) meat dish in a light, spicy sauce. As a starter, usually prepared with *galéo* (houndshark), or with *skórpios* (scorpion fish) or *pastanáka* (stingray) as a main course

▶ **briám** – a kind of ratatouille

▶ **chélia** – eel, grilled or in aspic: a Corfiot speciality (order in advance)

▶ **gópes** – grilled or fried sardines, often served as a snack

▶ **juvétsi** – noodle gratin with beef (occasionally, with lamb)

▶ **kokorétsi** – grilled offal wrapped in natural skin

▶ **marídes** – crisp, fried anchovies eaten head and all

▶ **nouboúlo** – speciality from the northwest of the island: lightly smoked pork (starter)

▶ **pastitsáda** – beef and chicken with noodles

▶ **patsária** – beetroot; cold as a salad or warm as a vegetable dish

▶ **sofríto** – beef, marinated in garlic and vinegar and braised in wine

▶ **spanakópitta** – puff pastry filled with spinach (photo, top left)

▶ **stifádo** – beef or rabbit stew in a tomato-cinnamon sauce

▶ **táramosaláta** – red puree of potatoes, soaked bread and fish roe (starter)

▶ **tirópitta** – puff pastry filled with cheese

▶ **tzizimbirra** – lemonade with a touch of ginger

Snack bars *psistariá* are a good alternative to restaurants for a quick bite. You can order chicken or pork *gýros* in *pita* bread or on a plate *(mérida)*, meatballs, local sausage and – quite often – chicken. Chips are omnipresent. You can find pizzerias in most of the holiday resorts, while other speciality restaurants are rare. But there are a few Chinese and Italian hostelries and many English pubs with genuine pub grub such as *steak & kidney pie* and *ploughman's lunch.*

Those with a sweet tooth will make their way to the *zácharoplastío*, the Greek pastry shop, with its mainly oriental specialities such as *baklavás* and *kataífi* ('angel's hair')

along with cream and sponge cakes. In addition to plain and simple water, you will often find wine from the barrel, and good restaurants usually have a wide variety of bottled wines – and an increasing number of organic wines. *Rétsina*, white wine flavoured with resin, is quite cheap and is popular in simple tavernas. The national alcoholic drink is *oúzo,* an aniseed schnapps that turns white when you add water to it. *Metaxá* brandy comes in various qualities – three, five and even seven stars – and is a good way to end a meal.

The Corfiot speciality ☺ *tzitzimbírra* is a non-alcoholic drink made of lemon juice, sugar, water and a touch of ginger. You can sample this from the beginning of May in villages such as Sokráki in the north of the island. It almost disappeared in the early 1990s but the demand created by the holidaymakers led to the traditional drink remaining on the market. If you order it, you are helping to preserve a tradition – and it is very tasty.

The Greeks drink coffee at any time of the day. However, ordering it in Greece is something of a science. You have the choice between a small cup of Greek coffee, *kafé ellenikó*, hot instant coffee, usually called *ness sestó*, cold, whipped instant coffee served with ice cubes, *frappé*, and the trendy *freddo* as either cappuccino or espresso. If you order Greek coffee, you must always say how sweet you want it because the ground coffee is mixed with sugar and then brewed: *skétto* is without, *métrio* with a little and *glikó* with a lot of sugar. And, of course, Greek coffee is always without milk. If you want to have your hot or cold Nescafe with milk you just have to add *mä gala*. On Corfu, the older people like to put a small shot of ouzo in their coffee and order *kafé elliniko mä poli úso mässa.*

Always busy: the cafés under Kérkyra's arcades

SHOPPING

You will find T-shirts with various sayings and motifs ironed on them everywhere. With the exception of gold and silver jewellery, hand-painted icons, ceramics, leather and some antiques, more sophisticated souvenirs are rare.

Most of the better shops are located in the town of Corfu where the locals also like to shop. However, they are more on the lookout for the latest fashions from Athens and Italy than Corfiot products. The Corfiots prefer to buy in boutiques, with a smaller range of quality goods, than in normal chain stores. Looking for a bargain? Then you should keep your eyes open during the first 20 days of August with the summer sales and discounts of up to 70%.

Opening hours: Shops are usually open from 8.30am to 2pm from Monday to Friday and from 6pm to 9pm on Tuesday, Thursday and Friday. Most supermarkets and souvenir shops are open from 8.30am to 11pm. You can buy last minute souvenirs in the departure hall of the airport – open round the clock.

ARTS & CRAFTS

Objects carved out of olive wood are really special: bowls, cups, salad servers, as well as small pieces of furniture such as stools and tables. You can find them in several shops in the Old Town of Corfu and in mountain villages including Makrádes, Lákones and Strinílas as well as the beach resort Acharávi. The best place to buy artistic glassware for your home is in Ágios Stéfanos Avliotón or in the Old Town of Corfu where there are also several antique shops.

CULINARY TREATS

If you want something really typical of the island, take some home-grown Corfiot products home with you. You can buy them at weekly markets, in private houses and *kafenía*, the small village shops and at roadside stands. In some places, you can buy thyme honey directly from the beekeeper. The best place to buy herbs from the island mountains is in Makrádes.

Nature provides the very best things – if you look around, you will discover delicious Corfiot specialities and beautiful arts and crafts

CUMQUATS

● Cumquats – little oranges, a maximum of 4 cm long, with a yellowy-orange skin – are a unique island speciality. The vitamin-rich citrus fruit is made into marmalade and liquor or sold as candied fruit. The latest trend is a newly-created eau de toilette with a fruity, tangy cumquat aroma.

MUSIC

Many souvenir shops sell CDs with Greek music à la Alexis Zorba at reasonable prices – although no Greek would ever buy them. If you are looking for good recordings of up-to-date Greek music of any kind, you should visit the special shops in the island's capital where you will get good advice and be able to listen to the music. Greeks often buy illicitly pressed CDs from hawkers – most of them from sub-Saharan Africa. They are illegal

and you have no way of checking their quality.

OLIVE OIL

Pure olive oil from Corfu tastes even better if you know which grove it has come from. However, the health standards now in force mean that you should only buy it in cans. Another delicious Corfiot speciality is olive paste – great as a dip or spread on bread. The olive-oil soap produced on the island can also be recommended.

WINE, LIQUEURS & SPIRITS

You can taste Corfiot wines, liqueurs and spirits in cellars and distilleries, as well as roadside booths before you buy them. However, it is usually difficult to transport wine.

THE PERFECT ROUTE

KÉRKYRA – 'ONE OF THE FAIREST OF THEM ALL'

Start your tour in ① *Kérkyra* → p. 32. The Greek beauty queen, which combines a touch of Venetian elegance with British eccentricity, lies on the coast and looks up to the high mountains. It invites you to shop, visit its churches and museums and any number of cafés, tavernas and restaurants.

VIEW FROM THE HIGHEST PEAK OF THE ISLAND

If you decide not to go for the refreshing waters of the seaside resorts near Corfu Town such as *Kontokáli*, *Gouviá* and ② *Dassiá* that stretch out as far as the foot of the *Pantokrátor* mountain range, drive from *Pírgi* via *Spartilas* to *Strinilas* → p. 59. After a short stop in the small tavern under an ancient elm tree, the route takes you up a twisting road with hairpin bends to the peak of ③ *Pantokrátor* → p. 58 (photo, left) at a height of 906 m (2972 ft). Drivers should have a good head for heights when trying to turn round!

DISCOVER THE NORTH COAST

Starting in ④ *Acharávi* → p. 48, drive along the north coast to *Sidári* → p. 54 and ⑤ *Cape Drástis* → p. 56. The view along the chalk cliffs is just as fantastic as the one out to sea where the tiny Diapontine Islands form stepping stones on the way to Italy.

DREAM BEACHES & PRIME OLIVE OIL

Enjoy a dip in the water from one of the long sandy beaches which are still devoid of large hotels, before continuing your tour. The narrow beach in *Peruládes* → p. 57 is drawn out along the steep coast; near *Ágios Stéfanos* it widens to as much as 100 m and runs for miles. When you stroll through ⑥ *Afiónas* → p. 55, the view of the bay of *Arillás* → p. 55 in the north and the wonderful sandy beach of *Ágios Geórgio Pagóns* → p. 55 in the south will make you feel like you are on a sky-walk. Before you carry on your journey, you should sample the excellent olive oil that can be found here.

SURREAL CASTLES & HEAVENLY VISTAS

The ⑦ *Angelókastro* → p. 66 hovers like an ethereal castle high above the sea, and the terraces of the cafés and tavernas in *Lákones* → p. 63 resemble heavenly balconies from which there is a wonderful view down to the olive trees and cypresses on *Paleokastrítsa* → p. 63. For many Corfiots, this is the most beautiful place on earth.

Discover the many different faces of Corfu on a two-day tour around the island which includes a few short detours to special sights

GET YOUR BREATH BACK AGAIN IN THE COUNTRYSIDE

Lush *Rópa Valley* gives you the chance to catch your breath after all the bends and ups and downs of the road. You will probably reach the former hippie village **8** *Pélekas* → p. 89, high above the valley, at just the right time – sunset. Let the day end here. Stroll to your hotel for the night or drive the short distance back to **1** *Kérkyra* → p. 32, just 13 km (8.1 mi) away.

FOLLOW IN THE FOOTSTEPS OF TWO ROYAL FIGURES

You will get the most out of Empress Elisabeth (Sisi)'s famous little castle **9** *Achíllion* → p. 47 (photo, left), where Emperor Wilhelm II also stayed, if you get up a bit earlier than usual and are there when it opens. When the crowds from the cruise ships arrive, you will already be in **10** *Lefkími* → p. 73 in the south with the islands most beautiful river port.

HIGH DUNES, A BIG LAKE AND A LONG BEACH

You will find a magnificent dune landscape near **11** *Ágios Geórgios Argirádon* → p. 68 with Corfu's largest stretch of inland water behind it, **12** *Lake Koríssion* → p. 70. The beach at its northern spit runs for miles and is almost deserted; the single taverna above the tiny port in

180 km (112 mi). Time: 5 hours. Detailed map of the route on the back cover, in the road atlas and the pull-out map.

Alonáki → p. 70 is probably the best and cosiest in the entire area. The centuries-old olive groves along the coastal road to *Paramónas* → p. 75 and **13** *Pendáti* → p. 75, with its panorama snack bar, are like an enchanted forest, and now you only have to drive back to town to finish your tour.

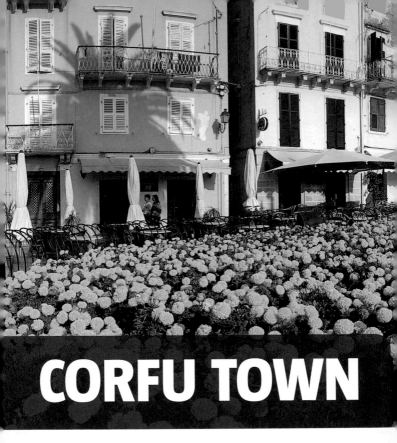

CORFU TOWN

WHERE TO START?
To reach the central **Esplanade** (U E–F 3–5) (𝑀 e–f 3–5), go up to **Plátia G. Theotókou** (Sarocco Square) from the long-distance bus terminal. This is also the terminus for busses to the nearby beaches. The **Odós G. Theotóki** that makes its way as **Odós Voulgaréos** through the Old Town will lead you to the open square between the **Old Fortress, Old Palace** and **Ionian Academy**. It is best to park your car at the **Old Harbour** (the Esplanade car park is often full) and then walk.

MAP INSIDE BACK COVER
The town of Corfu (Greek: *Kérkyra*) (127 E5–6) (𝑀 D5) is different from other Greek cities. Its architecture shows that the island was never Turkish but Venetian for 400 years and British for another 50. Corfu (population: 28,000) only became Greek again in 1864.

Two castles, the Old and New Fortresses, protected the Venetians and Greeks against a Turkish invasion for centuries. The Old Town, a Unesco World Heritage Site since 2007, lies between these two forts – its most beautiful section is the residential area of *Cambiéllo*. There, four and five-storey buildings, often with penthouses perched precariously on their roofs,

Photo: The Old Town of Kérkyra

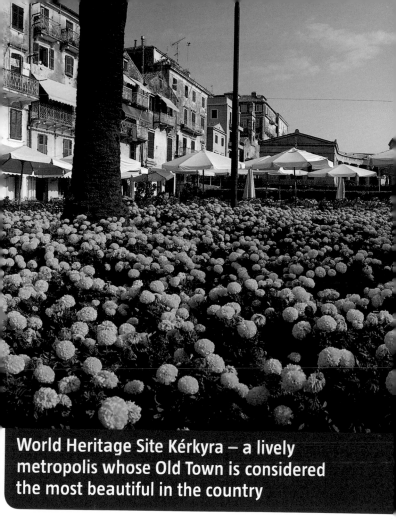

World Heritage Site Kérkyra – a lively metropolis whose Old Town is considered the most beautiful in the country

line the confusing labyrinth of streets with flapping laundry hung out to dry in the wind. Cats and dogs wander around and the bricks of the repeatedly repaired walls show behind the flaking plaster. An old archway can be seen here and there, with some houses decorated with pretty reliefs and small statues.

The most pleasant time to stroll through this district is early on Sunday morning when the bells are ringing and the Byzantine chant can be heard coming from the churches. The people on this island are real fans of classical music and sometimes you will hear Roman-Catholic church music coming from a tape or CD – that doesn't happen anywhere else in Greece!

The commercial area of the Old Town extends to the south and southwest of Cambiéllo. Rows of shops line the wide streets with their marble paving – very slippery when wet – and shady arcades that often lead into small squares; but the town's main 'living room' is the broad Esplanade in front of the Old Fortress with café after café. The Old Town is surrounded by modern housing areas. They are not the concrete jungles you often find in other parts of Greece; their avenues and

If you come by car, you will find parking near the Old Town at the Old Harbour *(1.50 euros/day)* and the Esplanade *(2 euros/day)*. You can rent a horse-drawn carriage in front of the Schulenberg Memorial on the Esplanade – or, during the day, at the Old Harbour – for your city tour *(approx. 30 euros/30 min)*.

The Old Fortress withstood many sieges; today, it is the symbol of Kérkyra

arcades give them an almost aristocratic air. The roofs are often tiled and gardens provide breathing space between the houses.

You should visit Kérkyra at least twice – once in the morning to stroll through the market and shopping district and visit the museums, churches and forts; and a second time in the late afternoon to promenade along the Esplanade, sit in a café and, later on, have dinner, like the Greeks, in a taverna in the Old Town. And there is no alternative at all to the island's capital if you want to go on a club or disco tour!

SIGHTSEEING

OLD FORTRESS
(U C5–6) (∭ c5–6)

The Byzantines and Venetians considered the rocky peninsula, with its two approximately 60 m-high hills in the east of the Old Town, the perfect place to build a fort. Until the 16th century, Kérkyra lay within its walls. The fort was protected on the land side by a moat, the *Contrafossa*, cut deep into the stone. Small fishing boats lie at anchor here and there are corrugated-iron huts that are used as weekend cottages and sheds on its fringe. There is a small exhibition of beautiful early-Christian mosaics from the Paleópolis Basilica in the gatehouse.

The most impressive building was erected by the British; it is St. George's Church (usually closed) with a façade modelled on a Doric temple. You have an unsurpassed view over the whole town from the front ⚘ peak of the peninsula. *April–Oct: Mon 1.30–8pm, Tue–Sun 8.30am–8pm, at other times: Tue–Sun 8.30am–3pm | Admission 4 euros (combined ticket, see p. 115), after that, free to 2am – without access to the peak*

OLD PALACE ●
(U F2) (*Ⅶ f2*)

The English had the largest building on the island constructed in classicistic style on the northern edge of the esplanade between 1819 and 1823 for the Lord High Commissioner of the islands. The sandstone used came from Malta, which the British had also appropriated. The Order of Saint George and Saint Michael that had recently been founded for officers who had rendered outstanding service on Malta and the Ionian Islands had its seat in this palace. Today, only a few rooms are open to the public but they give an idea of the splendour in which the British High Commissioner lived in the 19th century. *April–Oct: Mon 1.30–8pm, Tue–Sun 8.30am–8pm; at other times: Tue–Sun 8.30am–3pm | Admission 3 euros (combined ticket, see p. 115) | Esplanade*

ARCHAEOLOGICAL MUSEUM ★ ●
(U B6) (*Ⅶ b6*)

Most of the finds in the museum come from the ancient town of Kérkyra. The most valuable objects are the remains of two temple gables. The Archaic *Górgo Gable* dates from around 590 BC and had the function of keeping evil forces from the temple. From the front, it shows the kneeling Gorgon Medusa with her terrifying face, the sight of which turned the enemy to stone. The late-Archaic gable from around 510 BC shows figures from Greek mythology in profile. We can see the

---

MARCO POLO HIGHLIGHTS

God of wine, Dionysus, his son, Oinopion lying naked behind him, as well as a lion, a fragment of a dog and large wine 'kraters', a clay drinking vessel with two handles. The God Hephaestus, who made Dionysus drunk so that he could abduct him to the home of the Gods on Mount Olympus, was shown on the other half; unfortunately, this has not survived.

The early-Archaic statue of a reclining lion from around 630 BC is even older than the two gables and gives a clear impression of how Greek art attempted to free itself from the stiff, stylised form of its oriental models. *Tue–Sun 8.30am–3pm | Admission 3 euros (combined ticket, see p. 115) | Odós Wraíla 1*

ARTEMIS TEMPLE
(127 E6) (*ØD5*)

Unfortunately, there is little to see of the remains of the most important temple in ancient Kérkyra that were discovered in 1812. In spite of that, archaeologists determined that the temple had been built around 590 BC, was 48 m long and 22 m wide and that the main hall was formed of 48, more than 6 m high, columns. Only the 2.70 m wide and 25.4 m long sacrificial altar was well preserved. The first scientific excavations were made by the German classical scholar Wilhelm Dörpfeld with great support from Emperor Wilhelm II. *Admission free. Located in front of the walls of the Ágii Theodóri Monastery, access is from the Paleópolis Basilica over the Odós Derpfeld, continue left on the tarmac road after the first fork | City bus to Kanóni, Paleópolis stop*

PALEÓPOLIS BASILICA
(127 E6) (*ØD5*)

Towards the end of the 5th century, the early Christians on Corfu built a church

The gables in the Archaeological Museum tell a story of their own

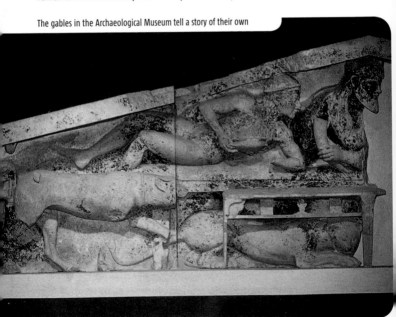

with five naves on top of the, still recognisable, remains of a small Roman music theatre, an 'Odeon', and traces can still be seen in the ground. Its floor was originally decorated with magnificent mosaics and some lovely fragments have been preserved in the exhibition rooms in the Old Fortress. The impressive walls come from a small, Gothic church from the Venetian period that included Antique elements. *Tue–Sun 8.30am–3pm | Admission free | Opposite the entrance to the Mon Repos Castle Park | City bus to Kanóni, Paleópolis stop*

BANKNOTE MUSEUM
(U E3) *(ɷ e3)*

The small, private museum in the Ionian Bank building displays banknotes from many countries and times and – intriguingly – even tells you how to make them! *April–Sept: Wed and Fri 9am–2pm and 5.30–8.30pm, Thur 9am–3pm, Sat/Sun 8.30am–3pm, at other times: Wed–Sun 8am–3pm | Admission free | Odós N. Theotóki*

INSIDER TIP ▶ BRITISH CEMETERY
(U A–B6) *(ɷ a–b6)* ●

The cemetery with its colonial tombstones seems like an enchanted park and it is not only a romantic place but also a great attraction for flower-lovers in spring and autumn with its many wild orchids. *Daily, from sunrise to sunset | Odós Kolokotróni 25*

BYZANTINE MUSEUM ★
(U D1) *(ɷ d1)*

More than 100 valuable icons from the 15th–18th centuries from Corfiot houses of worship have found a dignified new home in the *Panagía Antivuniótissa* Church in the Old Town. Soft Byzantine music can be heard in the background while you make your visit. Of the stories these icons tell, two are especially note-

worthy. The fourth icon on the left after the cash desk shows St. George on a horse with a young boy holding a teapot and cup sitting behind him. Pirates had abducted him and made him their cup-

Enchanted and peaceful:
the British Cemetery

bearer. In her sorrow, his mother turned to St. George who brought her son back to her. The icon to the left of the west portal is a work by the famous Cretan painter Michaíl Damáskinos from around 1752 in the so-called Cretan style, showing Saints Sérgios, Bákchos and Justini. It is felt that they were responsible for the Christian fleet defeating the Turks on their feast day, 7 October, in 1571. They are shown standing on a decapitated three-headed monster symbolising the Turkish fleet. *Tue–Sun 8.30am–3pm | Admission 2 euros (combined ticket, see p. 115) | Steps lead up from the Odós Arseníu*

THE ESPLANADE ⭐
(U E–F 3–5) *(𝄞 e–f 3–5)*

The broad expanse of the Esplanade fulfils the function of the *platía* (square) in other Greek cities: it is the centre of all social life, the site of the *vólta* – the traditional promenade held every evening – and occasional military parades; it is a meeting place for young and old, for the locals and holidaymakers. The Venetians created it in the 17th century. Until then, the houses in the town reached all the way to the Old Fortress. The army had them torn down to have the unrestricted possibility to open fire in the case of a siege. Later, this green area was used as a parade ground but today cricket is played on the grass. There is a fountain in the shady park. One of the monuments erected here commemorates the unification of the Ionian Islands with free Greece in 1864. It shows seven bronze reliefs with symbols of the seven main islands. Corfu is represented by the ship of the Phaeacians, the legendary people that – according to Homer – lived on Corfu and brought Odysseus back to his homeland of Ithaca by ship.

The west side of the Esplanade is flanked by tall, 19th-century houses that are still used for their original purpose today. It is lovely to sit in the little armchairs in one of the cafés under their arcades or *liston* – although it is quite pricey.

FALIRÁKI (ÁGIOS NIKÓLAS GATE)
(U F1) *(𝄞 f1)*

Today, the lovely building with the small St. Nicholas Chapel on a peninsula north of the Old Fortress is an ideal place to relax on the waterfront with a drink or have a delicious meal. In the 19th cen-

tury, this was where those travelling by the steam and sailing-ships anchored at the docks, which was often where emigrants departed for America, went on board or disembarked. *Usually 8pm–2am (as long as the bars are open) | Free access from Odós Arseníu*

CEMETERY CHURCH
(127 E6) *(𝄞 D5)*

Three valuable icons by the Cretan painter Michail Damáskinos from the late 16th century hang in the church of the town's main cemetery that was built in 1840. They show Christ as the high priest, Maria and Saint Anthony. *Daily 7.30am–5.30pm | Anemómilos district, entrance from Odós Anapáseos*

KÁNONI, VLACHÉRNA MONASTERY AND PONTIKONÍSSI ☆
(127 E6) *(𝄞 D 5–6)*

The lookout point at the tip of the Análipsis Peninsula takes its name from a canon from the Napoleonic era. The ● view to the two little islands off the coast, Vlachérna and Pontikoníssi, is the epitome of the Corfiot picture postcard. Vlachérna can be reached over a small sea wall and is almost entirely taken up by the monastery that was built around 1700 – now no longer in use. A boat sets out from the sea wall to the 'Mouse Island' (the translation of Pontikoníssi) where Austria's Empress 'Sisi' liked to sit. The small church was built in the 12th century. *Monastery and church open to the public during the day*

KARDÁKI SPRING
(127 E6) *(𝄞 D5)*

A short stroll along a narrow path at the edge of the Mon Repos castle park takes you from the Análipsis district down to this Venetian spring. Its water used to flow out of the head of a Lion of St Mark. *Free access | The path begins at* the square-like space in front of the church and cemetery of Análipsis between houses 14 and 18

ÁGIOS JÁSON KE SOSSÍPATROS CHURCH (127 E6) *(ltl D5)*

This thousand-year-old, cross-vaulted church is the most splendid example of Byzantine architecture on Corfu. The lower section of the walls was built out of tuff, regularly hewn in ancient times; further up, the ashlars are separated by decorative rows of bricks – the eastern wall is especially impressive. Here, the bricks are arranged in the style of the Cufic characters popular in the Arab world to form the letters IC – the monogram for Jesus Christ. *Admission free | Anemómilos district | City bus to Kanóni, Jáson ke Sossípatro stop*

ÀGIOS SPIRÍDONAS CHURCH ●

(U E2–3) *(ltl e2–3)*

Believers have showered the church of the island's patron saint, which is located in the centre of the Old Town, with votive offerings. Its most precious relics are the bones of St Spiridon, a Cypriot martyr from around 300 AD. Corfu purchased these relics in 1456 and it is said that the saint has performed countless major and minor miracles over the centuries.

The interior of the church was completely redecorated in the 18th and 19th centuries in the style of the Ionian school – the ceiling paintings and icons are no longer in keeping with the Byzantine tradition but are orientated totally on models from the west. St Spiridon's silver-embossed, ebony sarcophagus is in the side chapel on the right, behind the iconostasis. Believers of all age groups come throughout the day, light a candle, kiss the sarcophagus and write their wishes or thanks to the saint in a book. Silver oil lamps, donated by believers, hang over the sarcopha-

The tower of Ágios Spirídonas Church

gus. It is easy to recognise that some of them were donated by seamen and ship owners: they are decorated with silver model boats or with votive plates of ship reliefs. *Open during the day | Odós Spirídonos*

PANAGÍAS SPILIÓTISSIS KE ÁGION VLASIÚ KE THEODÓRAS (MITRÓPOLIS) CHURCH (U D2) (🗺 d2)

The locals call 'All Saints Church of the Cave and the Saints Blase and Theodora' the Mitrópolis – Bishop's Church – for short. Its greatest treasure are the bones of the Byzantine Empress Theodora that lie in a silver sarcophagus in the chapel to the left of the sanctuary. The Empress is of great importance for the Orthodoxy because she put an end to a Civil War in the Byzantine Empire that had lasted for more than a century, the Ikonoklasmos, in 843 AD. This was fought over the holiness of icons and the justification for worshiping them.

Empress Theodora saw that those in favour of pictures won and, without her, there would be no icons in Orthodox churches today. For this reason, many of those in the Mitrópolis show her holding one. *Daily, at least from 7.30am–1pm and 4.30–8.00pm | Old Town | Odós Vitzarú Kiriakí | Entrance from the Old Harbour*

AGÍAS EFTHÍMIAS CONVENT (127 E6) (🗺 D5)

This convent from the Venetian era is particularly notable for its beautiful inner courtyard with its many flowers. *In summer: open daily 8am–1pm and 4–8pm; at other times: 9am–noon and 4–6pm | Anemómilos district | On the road from Mon Repos beach to the Paleópils Basilica*

ÁGII THEODÓRI CONVENT (127 E6) (🗺 D5)

Next to the site of the Antique Artemis Temple, this convent with its large atmospheric courtyard is a place of silence. The remains of an early-Christian basilica were integrated into the convent church; other sections of the complex are, however, closed to visitors. *Daily 9am–1pm and 5–7.30pm (ring the bell if the gate is closed) | City bus to Kanóni, Paleópolis stop and then follow the path to Artemis Temple*

KREMASTI FOUNTAIN (U D2) (🗺 d2)

A private benefactor donated this fountain to the city 'for the well-being of the general public' (according to the inscription). It is located at one of the loveliest places in the Cambiéllo district of the Old Town. *Platía Lili Desilla, can be reached via Odós Ágias Theodóras*

MON REPOS ⭐ (127 E6) (🗺 D5)

The small castle with its somewhat overgrown park has a turbulent tale to tell.

LOW BUDGET

▶ If you choose the right day, many of the sights in the town can be visited free of charge. Entrance to the Archaeological **(U B6)** *(🗺 b6)* and Byzantine Museums **(U D1)** *(🗺 d1)*, the Old Palace **(U F2)** *(🗺 f2)* and the Old Fortress **(U C5–6)** *(🗺 c5–6)* is free every Sunday in winter, as well as on the first Sunday in April, May and October, on all public holidays, 6 March, the last weekend in September, World Museum Day in May, on World Memorial Day on 18 April and on World Environment Day on 5 June.

▶ Feel like fast food? The greatest choice can be found on the Esplanade **(U E–F4)** *(🗺 e–f4)* at the west end of Odós Dousmáni; Many typical gyros taverns can be found in the streets parallel to Odós Zaitsainóu near the Old Harbour **(U C2)** *(🗺 c2)*.

The British Lord High Commissioner had it built as his private residence and it was taken into the possession of the Greek royal family in 1864. In 1921, Prince Philip, Queen Elizabeth II's husband, was born here. Since 2001, the castle has served as the museum for the history of Paleópolis. A INSIDER TIP 10 minute walk through the almost tropical park with its old trees will take you to the idyllic *Doric temple* from the 5th century BC at the end of the signposted path. *Park open daily 8am–7pm | Admission free; museum Tue–Fri 8.30am–3pm | Admission 3 euros | Entrance at the Paleópolis stop on the bus route to Kanóni.*

MUSEUM OF ASIAN ART
(U F2) (*m̄ f2*)

Artworks from many Asian countries, which a Greek diplomat donated to the state, are exhibited in many rooms in the Old Palace. Most of them come from Japan, Korea, India, Tibet, Thailand, Burma and China. *April–Oct: Mon 1.30–8pm, Tue–Sun 8.30am–8pm; at other times: Tue–Sun 8.30am–3pm | Admission 3 euros (combined ticket, see p. 115)*

NEW FORTRESS (NÉO FRÚRIO) ⬌
(U A–B 2–3) (*m̄ a–b 2–3*)

The New Fortress occupies a hill-top site between the old and new ports. It is not at all new, only not quite as old as the Old Fortress. The Venetians built it in the 16th century. The port gate with the relief of St Mark's lion is very beautiful and the long, dark passages inside the castle are extremely impressive as is the fine panoramic view from the roof of the citadel. There is also an exhibition of the history of Corfiot ceramics from ancient times to the present day. *June–Sept: daily 9am–10pm; at other times: 9am–5pm | Admission 3 euros | Entrance Odós Solomú*

Tropical greenery – in the park of Mon Repos Castle

TOWN HALL
(U D3–4) (*m̄ d3–4*)

The ground floor of the harmoniously designed building was built in the late 17th century as a clubhouse for the Venetian nobility. In 1721, it was converted into a theatre and, in 1903, into the town hall. *The interior is not open to the public | Platía Dimarchíu*

ROMAN-CATHOLIC CATHEDRAL AGÍU IAKÓVU KE CHRISTOPHÓRU

U E4) (*m e4*)

The church, with its Classicist façade, was built in 1553, but was subjected to major alterations in 1658 and partially destroyed by German incendiary bombs in 1943. It was not re-consecrated until 1970. *Usually open throughout the day | Mass, June–Sept: Sat 7pm, Sun 8.30am, 10am and 7pm; Oct–May: 6pm instead of 7pm | Platía Dimarchíu*

Venetian service – successfully defended Corfu from the Turks, is located near the bridge to the Contrafossa that leads into the Old Fortress. *Esplanade*

VÍDOS

(127 E5) (*m D5*)

The lush, green island located so close to the town is ideal for a gentle stroll. There is also a small pebble beach that is mainly frequented by the locals and a mausoleum dedicated to those soldiers of the

The Esplanade in Kérkyra is atmospheric in the evening

CITY ART GALLERY (U F2) (*m f2*)

Most of the works in the collection of paintings in two side wings of the Old Palace were created by Corfiot painters from the 19th and 20th centuries. *Daily 9am–9pm | Admission 1 euro*

SCHULENBERG MEMORIAL

(U F4) (*m f4*)

A baroque memorial to Count Johann Matthias von der Schulenberg, who – in

Serbian Army who fell on Corfu during World War I. *(In summer, small ferries take passengers to and from Vídos from the Old Port; 10am–midnight, on the hour).*

The ● *Calypso Star* makes 40-minute tours around the island of Vídos every hour between 10am and 6pm. Passengers can stand in the ship's hull and watch the submarine world through large windows. *(Departure from the same jetty at the Old Port | 14 euros).*

FOOD & DRINK

AEGLI (U E2) (*m e2*)

Classical restaurant and café right on the Esplanade with tables both indoors and outside. International and Greek cuisine – the patron is the German honorary consul on the island and makes sure that the restaurant's reputation is upheld. *Daily after 10am | Expensive*

ALÉKOS BEACH ☆

(U F2) (*m f2*)

Nowhere else on Corfu can you eat closer to the water. Sometimes the waves even splash over the quay when the ferries pass by – then everybody leaps up to keep their feet dry! The view of the floodlit Old Fortress and port building in Faliráki in the evening is particularly atmospheric. Small skewers of meat – *souvláki* – cost around 1.70 euros each and you have to decide on how many you want when you order. *Daily | Faliráki | Ágios Nikólas Gate | Budget*

INSIDER TIP BELLISSIMO

(U D3)(*m d3*)

Father and son, Kóstas and Stávros, take care of the service. Ánna and Dóra are in charge of the kitchen. There are five to six different specialities every day along with gyros and grilled meat. Spanakópitta, home made puff pastry filled with chard, mint, leek, a bit of cheese and touch of fennel, is pure poetry. Meals are served on a pretty, newly laid-out square. *Mon–Sat, and Sunday evenings in August | Odós D. Bitzárou Kyriaki | Entrance between 67 and 69 Odós N. Theotóki | Budget*

INSIDER TIP DIMARCHIO

(U E4) (*m e4*)

The main selling point of this restaurant on the square in front of the town hall is its size. Greek and Mediterranean cooking with delicious fish dishes at set prices. *Daily | Platía Dimarchíu | Corner of Odós Guilford | Expensive*

EKTÓS SKÉDIO

(U C2) (*m c2*)

This *tsipourádiko* is popular with the locals all year round. As the name tells you, this is where *tsípouro* – a kind of grappa – is served. There are other drinks as well and an enormous selection of Greek specialities, served as small portions so that you can put together your personal feast. Holiday-makers are welcome but not wooed. Most of the visitors are young, fairly well off Corfiots which means that things get lively after 10pm. *Daily, only in the evening | Odós Prossaléndiou 43 | Behind the Court building | Moderate*

EY LOUNGE ●

(U E3) (*m e3*)

Lounge, café and restaurant. This is the place for a good breakfast, pasta, salads, warm and cold snacks, as well as international dishes. Corfiot business people meet here for lunch; in the evening, the lounge is the perfect venue to start the night. *Daily | Odós Kapodistríu 32 | Expensive*

OLD FORTRESS CAFÉ ★

(U C6) (*m c6*)

The modern café in the Old Fortress is an atmospheric location to drink excellent Greek wines, cocktails or *tsípouro* (grappa) accompanied by an omelette, salad, or platter of mixed starters, *pikilies*. There are concerts on some evenings. *Daily | In the Old Fortress | Admission only with a valid ticket when the Old Fortress is open; after that, free | Expensive*

INSIDER TIP PÉRGOLA ☺

(U C3)(*m c3*)

Sákis, the owner of this unpretentious taverna, serves the best Greek food, slightly sparkling wine from the village of

Zitsa on the mainland and excellent grappa. Stuffed aubergines with a cheese topping and his salad of wild greens *tsigarélli* are heavenly. *Daily | Odós Agías Sofías 10 | Moderate*

ROÚVAS
(U C4) (🛍 c4)

There is no outdoor seating in this typical market taverna, but here you can choose your meal directly from the pots of – mostly – stewed dishes. The salads are fresh and crisp, and the vegetables and meat come from the market. Many stall holders eat here – they know what quality is! *Mon–Sat | Odós Dessíla 13 | Budget*

TO PARADOSIAKÓN
(U C2) (🛍 c2)

Simple restaurant with reserved – but friendly – service by the young owner. Good for a quick lunch; you can also take a look in the kitchen. *Daily | Odós Solmú 20 | Moderate*

SHOPPING

The main shopping street for the locals is Odós Vuláréos in the Old Town and its continuation, ● Odós G. Theotóki, in the new section with its beautiful arcades. Modern shops, especially those selling electrical items and multimedia, can be found on the wide Odós Aléxandras that runs from Platía G. Theotóki (Sarocco Square) to the sea. Arts and crafts and souvenirs are mainly offered on Odós N. Theotóki, Odós Filarmonikís and Odós Filéllinon in the Old Town.

INSIDER TIP BY TOM ● 🙂
(U C2) (🛍 Xc2)

The olive-wood carver Thomás Koumarákos's unsophisticated workshop. Thomás still only uses traditional techniques and has been putting his heart and soul into his work since he started in 1969. He also makes bespoke pieces for his customers – quickly and at a reasonable price – and delights in showing them the hundreds of tools he uses. *31 Parodós N. Theotóki | Entrance between the houses at 81 and 83 Odós N. Theotóki*

GREEK MUSHROOMS 🙂
(U C4) (🛍 c4)

The small town of Grévena is famous throughout the region for its mushrooms. Even most Greeks are not aware of the extent of the mushroom gatherers' inventiveness and this can now be seen in this shop for the first time. Along with various kinds of dried mushrooms and noodles, you can even find them preserved in oil or bottled as mushroom liqueur! Grévena also produces berry liqueur and jam. *Odós Agias Sofías*

LALAÓUNIS
(U E3) (🛍 e3)

Greece's most renowned jeweller not only has branches in New York and on the Virgin Islands, but also in Corfu's Old Town. *Odós Kapodistríu 35 | On the northwest corner of the arcades on the Esplanade*

ROLÁNDOS
(U C2) (🛍 c2)

Paintings by the young owner Rolándos Roditis and his mother Marie – even including some on old ship planks. Also, ceramics from the village of Kinopiástes. *Odós N. Theotóki 99*

PATOÚNIS SOAP FACTORY ●
(U A6) (🛍 a6)

You can see how olive-oil soap is made in this more-than-hundred-year-old soap factory – and buy it in lovely wrappings. *Mon–Sat 9am–2pm; Tue, Thur, Fri also 5–8.30pm | Odós I. Teotóki 9 | www.patounis.gr*

VASSILÁKIS ★ ● 😊 (U E2) (*🗺 e2*)

The city shop of Corfu's largest distillery offers many types of cumquat liqueur as well as other varieties, and ouzo and brandy. Of course, you can taste before you buy. The latest creation is an eau-de-cologne with a touch of cumquat. *Daily 8am–midnight | Odós Spirídonos 61*

The small INSIDER TIP ► *Mon Repos* beach, with its popular *Kafeníon*, is the town's only beach *(daily, from 8am | Admission 1.50 euros)*. There are ladders at *Alékos Beach* on the Faliráki Promontory to provide better access to the water *(daily*

Liqueurs in pretty bottles are not the only attraction at Vassilákis' in Kérkyra

WEEKLY MARKET ★ 😊

(U B4) (*🗺 b4*)

A real market! You won't find any souvenirs here, but things the locals need every day: fresh fish and pulses, nuts, fruit and vegetables, herbs and flowers. There are small cafés between the stands and the proprietors even take coffee to the dealers; lottery ticket sellers promise high winnings. *Mon–Sat 7am–2pm | In the moat beneath Odós Sp. Vlaikoj*

8am–8pm | Admission 1.50 euros). The *Holiday Palace* next to the Kanóni lookout point offers a water-sport centre and four bowling alleys *(tel. 26 61 03 65 40)*.

CASINO (127 E6) (*🗺 D5*)

Roulette, blackjack and gaming machines. *Daily | Admission 7 euros | Hotel Holiday Palace | Kanóni*

CAVALIERI ROOF GARDEN ★ ☀
(U E5) (*ID e5*)

You have a wonderful view over the town and island all the way to the mountains in Albania from the **INSIDER TIP** roof garden of the Hotel Cavalieri. They not only serve all kinds of cocktails and drinks, but also sundaes, apple and lemon cakes, lasagne and crêpes filled with cheese and mushrooms. The roast pork stuffed with plums and apples is a real treat. *Daily | No admittance in shorts | Lift | Odós Kapodistríu 4 | Expensive*

DISCO TOUR (127 E5) (*ID D5*) ●

Corfu's latest nightlife district is located on the coast road near the ferry port and the adjacent first section of the road towards Kontokáli where there is an endless line of clubs. They rarely open before 11pm and there is usually a charge for live events and guest DJs. Long drinks cost from 7 to 10 euros. Under 17-year-olds are not allowed. The 'in' discos at the moment are modelled on those in Athens and are right next to each other on the road to Kontokáli: *Romeo & Juliet* and *Villa Mercedes* (mainly house, r&b, Greek pop, *admission in both: 12 euros*), the *Au Bar*, which caters to a considerably younger crowd (more Greek music) and the *Elektron* (almost only Greek rock and pop) where many like to take a nightcap.

WHERE TO STAY

BELLA VENEZIA ★
(U D5) (*ID d5*)

Atmospheric hotel in a Classicist building from the 19th century that was formerly a bank and then a school for girls. Each room is different and most have small balconies. Breakfast is served in the garden pavilion; the small bar opposite is the place to have an apéritif or nightcap in a relaxed environment. *32 rooms | Odós Zambelíu 4 | tel. 26 61 04 65 00 | www.bellaveneziahotel.com | Expensive*

INSIDER TIP CAVALIERI
(U E5) (*ID e5*)

Elegant hotel in a Venetian *palazzo* at the end of the Esplanade. *48 rooms | Odós Kapodistríu 4 | tel. 26 61 03 90 41 | www.cavalieri-hotel.com | Expensive*

CORFU PALACE (U B6) (*ID b6*)

Luxury hotel near the Old Town and sea with a seawater swimming pool, children's pool and indoor pool. You can reach the beaches by taxi or public bus. *106 rooms | Leofóros Dimokratías | tel. 26 61 03 94 85 | www.corfupalace.com | Expensive*

HERMES (U C4) (*ID c4*)

Simple hotel, centrally located near the market below the New Fortress. *32 rooms | Odós G. Markorá 14 | tel. 26 61 03 92 68 | www.hermes-hotel.gr | Budget*

INSIDER TIP KONSTANTINOÚPOLIS
(U C1) (*ID c1*)

Friendly hotel on five floors of a house built in 1861 directly by the Old Harbour. The reception and breakfast room are on the first floor; the small lobby between the two is like the salon of a traditional, middle-class Corfiot house. In spite of its age, the hotel's lift has always been reliable. *34 rooms | Odós K. Zavitsianoú 1 | tel. 26 61 04 87 16 | www.konstantinoupolis.gr | Moderate*

INFORMATION

TOURIST INFORMATION
(127 E6) (*ID D5*)

The information booth in the arrival hall of the airport is only sporadically manned in the summer months; no telephone or written information.

WHERE TO GO

ACHÍLLION ⭐
(128 B2) (*D6*)

Corfu's most popular excursion destination is a small castle high above the east coast in the middle of a magnificent park with many sculptures. Empress Elisabeth of Austria (1837–98), better known as 'Sisi', had it built and visited it many times from 1891 until her assassination in Geneva. In 1907, the German Emperor Wilhelm II bought the property and spent Easter

and lance. There are other statues showing the muses and many busts of ancient philosophers on the upper terrace.

You can visit the ground floor of Achíllion with its magnificent painted staircase, the castle chapel and several other rooms with furniture, paintings and other artefacts that remind one of the Imperial majesties. A particular oddity is Kaiser Wilhelm's desk chair in the shape of a saddle that sways like a rocking horse. *May–Oct: daily 8.30am–8pm; at other times: Tue–Sun 9am–4pm | Admission 7 euros*

Achíllion: Corfu's most famous sight and a place of refuge for imperial rulers

there every year. Achilles, the hero of the ancient sagas, was a favourite of the two royal figures, both putting up – completely different – monuments to him in the castle park. The melancholic Austrian loved the 'dying Achilles' with the arrow in his heel, while the Prussian admired the 'victorious Achilles' with his shield

You can taste the wines and liqueurs made by the *Vassilákis* distillery opposite Achíllion. *There are four to six buses daily to Achíllion – more in the high season – from San Rocco Square (line 10); tickets, also for the return trip, must be purchased in advance at the bus station or a kiosk; tickets are not available on the bus | 8 km (5 mi) from Kérkyra*

THE NORTH

A mighty mountain stretches all the way across Corfu between Paleokastrítsa and Kassiópi, probably the island's most beautiful coastal villages. The highest point is Pantokrátor and its upper regions are really alpine in character.

Serpentine roads lead to peaceful mountain villages, unmade tracks are a challenge to 4×4 drivers and mountain bikers. With its many old villages among the olive groves, the countryside in the northwest is more gentle. This is where herbs are sold and you can even enjoy wine tasting on the roadside. Panorama restaurants and a medieval castle offer wonderful views. There are also beaches for all tastes: mile-long stretches of fine sand in front of a flat hinterland or steep cliffs, small pebbly bays that can often only be reached by boat (and you do not need a license to rent one), and smooth chalk cliffs that you have to clamber down. The rustic cafés and idyllic village squares are the places to take a break and have a chat with the locals.

ACHARÁVI & RÓDA

(126–127 C–D 1–2) (*C2*) Acharávi and Róda lie about 3 km (1.9 mi) apart on the north coast of Corfu but they are linked

Photo: Cliffs near Sidári

Long beaches and the highest mountain – the north is where Corfu shows its impressive variety best

to each other by a 6 km (3.7 mi) long beach which is mostly fine sand.

Acharávi (pop. 650) was originally a fishing village with its historical centre lying inland some 500 m from the coast; the old heart of Róda (pop. 370) is directly on the shore. Today, both are lively holiday destinations in the summer months. Acharávi has more shops, tavernas and top-class hotels; Róda's advantage is its – very short – promenade along the shore.

As is often the case in Greece, you won't find any street names in these two villages. Orientation in Róda is quite simple; everything is concentrated around the coastal road and the short stretch connecting it to the island's main road network. The old main road leading to the centre of Acharávi, that was once just a small village, is off a rather nondescript roundabout located on the road around the island.

Pre-season – but even later there'll be enough room for everyone on the beach in Acharávi

SIGHTSEEING

ROMAN BATHS

In 1985, archaeologists unearthed the scanty remains of a Roman thermal bath. Experts can just about recognise the hypocaust floor supports. Hot air from an oven circulated between them – an early form of underfloor heating. *Free viewing | Acharávi | left, on the main road to Róda*

FOOD & DRINK

MONOLITHI

Romantically decorated taverna in a former olive mill on a green hill above Acharávi. Many northern-Greek specialities. Occasionally live music on Saturday and Sunday evenings. *Daily, from 11am | Signpost off the main road | Expensive*

PÁNGALOS ☆

Tables on the terrace of the more than 175-year-old warehouse are right on the shore. No other restaurant in Róda has a better location but the food is – like everywhere else in Róda – mediocre at best. *Daily, from 10am | Róda | On the coastal road in the village centre | Moderate*

PUMPHOUSE

A real restaurant with real tablecloths, the glow of tea light candles, fresh flowers on the table and easy-listening music in the background. Add to this, multilingual, fast, polite service and fine cooking. Many dishes are served with tasty roast potatoes and the well-spiced *tas kebab*, a kind of stew with three types of meat, is outstanding. Large portions. *Daily, from 5pm | Acharávi | At the roundabout | Expensive*

SHOPPING

OLIVE WOOD 😃

Large selection of olive-wood objects worked on the lathe by the owner Polychrónis himself, presented with charm by his Dutch wife Paulien. *On the road from the Dimítra Supermarket to the beach*

SPORT & BEACHES

The more than 6 km (3.7 mi) long beach of fine sand, with only a few pebbly patches, begins in Róda, makes its way past Acharávi and continues as *Almirós Beach* to the small island of *Agia Ekaterini* which can be reached over a footbridge. A 30-minute walk along a track will take you across the island to *Ágios Spirídonas* and, after another 15 minutes, you will reach the road around the island. You can then catch the bus back to Acharávi or Róda.

Guided two-hour tours on horseback are offered daily at 9am, 11am, 5pm and 7pm in Róda. The horses can be seen in a paddock on the road connecting the route around the island with the shore promenade.

There are water-sport facilities at the port in Róda and in front of the large hotels in Acharávi.

ENTERTAINMENT

HARRY'S BAR

Harry has been taking special care of his guests since 1981 and promotes communication at a reasonable price. You can watch all major sporting events on a large screen. *Acharávi | At the east end of the old village road | www.harrysbar-corfu.com*

INSIDER TIP LEMON GARDEN

The most unusual restaurant in the north of the island is a place where guests of all ages and whole families gather under old lemon trees or an aromatic, traditional Corfiot wooden roof for breakfast, a drink or meal. Meat and fresh fish are grilled every day in the garden and you will almost feel like you are at a private garden party. You won't find many places as atmospheric and personal as here *(Restaurant: Moderate). Acharávi | On the main road, 50 m to the west of the roundabout*

VEGGERA BEACH BAR

Lounge atmosphere between cacti and agaves in the beach bar that becomes a mecca for sunset freaks in the evening. *Acharávi | Access from the EuroHire travel agency on the main road*

MARCO POLO HIGHLIGHTS

YAMAS

Lacking a real discotheque, this small music bar with the apt name 'Cheers!' has become the evening meeting place for young holidaymakers and locals alike. *Daily | Acharávi | At the roundabout*

WHERE TO STAY

ACHARÁVI BEACH

Beach hotel with five one and two-storey buildings. Beach bar and pool between the hotel and beach. Rows of oleanders, lemon trees and palms decorate the garden. *97 rooms and apartments | Acharávi | East of the roundabout | tel. 26 63 06 31 02 | www.acharavibeach.com | Moderate*

LTI-GELÍNA VILLAGE

Spacious, all-inclusive complex with a large fun pool directly on the beach. Many sports activities, open-air cinema, spa facilities with indoor pool. *281 studios and apartments | At the eastern edge of the village | tel. 26 63 06 40 00 | www.gelinavillage.gr | Expensive*

INSIDER TIP ▶ RÓDA INN

Simple hotel and good value for money on the little used coastal road in Róda, only 10 m from the sandy beach. The very friendly owner, Helen, lives in Canada in winter and speaks English; most of the regular guests are British retirees. *25 rooms | Róda | tel. 26 63 06 33 58 | Budget*

SAINT GEORGE'S BAY COUNTRY CLUB ● ☺

This beach hotel is a perfect example of how best to adapt to the natural and historical surroundings. The seventy apartments, each accommodating up to four, are spread over a number of individually designed two-storey, island-style houses. Here, you almost feel that you are in a Corfiot village but with all mod cons and facilities. These include two flood-lit tennis courts, a clubhouse and restaurant, a spa area and large pool. *Acharávi | East of the roundabout | tel. 26 63 06 32 03 | www.stgeorgesbay.com | Expensive*

TOURIST STUDIO

Élena Vláchou's travel agency on the cul-de-sac leading to the Ionian Princess Hotel can arrange holiday apartments and houses in Acharávi. *Tel. 26 63 06 35 24*

WHERE TO GO

AGÍA EKATERÍNII (127 D1) (Ⓜ C2)

The northeast tip of Corfu is formed by the island of Agía Ekateríni that is covered by ferns and forests of pine, cypress and eucalyptus trees. On the landside, it is enclosed by Antoniótis, a lake of brackish water that is rich in fish, and the two arms connecting it to the sea. Bridges lead to the island; the one from Archarávi may only be used by pedestrians, cyclists and moped riders; the one to Ágios Spirídonas is also open to cars.

The deserted *Agía Ekateríni* (also written: *Ayia Aikaterini*) Monastery from 1713 lies hidden in a wood. Although there is not a lot to see, for those who want to, leave the track where it enters the wood and go straight ahead for two minutes.

Small paths also lead off of the main one to small, almost deserted, shingle beaches where nude bathing is possible. However, the 100-metre-long INSIDER TIP ▶ sandy beach at *Ágios Spirídonas* is much nicer; its gentle incline also makes it suitable for small children. There is a new, rather nondescript chapel and the Lagoon Taverna *(daily | Moderate)* that serves fresh fish on the beach. *8 km (5 mi) from Archarávi*

ASTRAKÉRI (126 C1) (Ⓜ B2)

The tiny hamlet with its houses scattered through an olive grove and a long beach

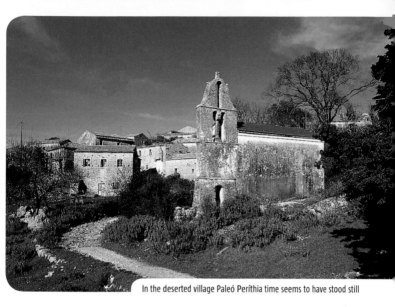

In the deserted village Paleó Períthia time seems to have stood still

of coarse sand is well known for the **INSIDER TIP** *Gregóris* tavern only 20 metres from the water. The live lobsters, caught by the proprietor, are less expensive than elsewhere *(signposted | Moderate)*. *6 km (3.7 mi) from Róda*

NÍMFES (126 C2) (*ⓜ C3*)

The **INSIDER TIP** *Evstrámenou Church*, which is unique in the world and continues to baffle historians, is located on the outskirts of Nímfes and can only be visited from outside. A dome similar to that of a Ceylonese stupa – a form of Buddhist temple – rises up over a hexagonal base. It is crowned by a hexagonal lantern of six windows. The church was probably erected in the 18th century but the white extension with the four-sided lantern and bell tower was not added until 1860.

The centre of the village lies on the edge of a valley with many cumquat trees. The simple taverns *(Budget)* are only open in the evening – except in August when they open earlier. *Left on the road from Plátonas to Nímfes (signposted) | 6 km (3.7 mi) from Róda*

PALEÓ PERÍTHIA ★ (127 E2) (*ⓜ D3*)

Paleó Períthia looks like a museum village from the Venetian period. Situated in a fertile, high-altitude valley below Pantokrátor, it was quite well-off in former days as can be seen by the large, sturdy stone houses and churches. However, its inhabitants moved down to the coast where they founded *Néa Períthia* (New Períthia). Only a few elderly shepherds remained. The village fell into oblivion and escaped the cementing boom of the 1970s and 80s. In the early 1990s, the first tavern opened and, today, there are four. The locals like the *Taverna Fóros* best – also **INSIDER TIP** because of its excellent walnut cake. *Buses only twice a day to Loútses, then 3 km (1.9 mi) on foot | 15 km (9.3 mi) from Archarávi*

ACHARÁVI & RÓDA

SIDÁRI (126 B1–2) (*𝄞 B 2*)

Sidári is like a fairground. There is a string of bars, travel agencies and souvenir shops along the main street; nothing is left of its former charm. The lingua franca is only Greek in winter; in summer, everyone speaks English. The pools are flooded with rock music and there is hardly a bar that doesn't have a large screen for sporting events.

chair hire operator also offers INSIDERTIP short motorboat trips under the sheer cliffs along the coast.

In Sidári (pop. 400) itself, you can rent a taxi-boat to take you along the coast or a pedal boat to at least get a closer look at some of the nearby areas under your own steam. If you don't rent a boat, you should walk or drive from the bridge over the stream towards Peruládes and turn off

Umbrellas, sunbeds and paddle boats can be hired on the beach at Sidári

Sidári might not be everybody's first choice for a holiday but it is worth visiting. Corfu's impressive, light-coloured cliffs that stretch around *Cape Drástis* past the small village of Peruládes, begin to the west of the stream that separates Sidári from the parish of Peruládes. Good swimmers can reach the water over the smooth rocks at the cape and the deck-

the small road to the Pool Bar Restaurant *Kahlua* at the ★ 🌿 *Canal d'Amour*. Here, the coast is not yet as steep and inaccessible as it becomes further westwards and there are even deckchairs and sunshades on the cliffs. These cliffs are lined with small bays and drowned valleys with short sandy beaches and a number of caves. *8 km (5 mi) from Róda*

ÁGIOS GEÓRGIOS, AFIÓNAS & ARILLÁS

(126 A–B 2–3) (*🗺 A3*) **Ágios Geórgios, which is actually part of the parish of Pági located further inland, and Arillás are coastal villages with long sandy beaches, while Afiónas is a mountain village on the peninsula separating the other two.** Ágios Geórgios and Arillás only come alive in summer but Afiónas exudes a delightful rural atmosphere, making it worth visiting on your way round the island. There are no major sights in any of the three villages but the surroundings of Arillás in particular attract many holidaymakers who want to do yoga and meditate.

FOOD & DRINK

'DAS BLAUE HAUS' 🕐 (THE BLUE HOUSE)

The owner serves excellent open wines, including some from Crete and Neméa on the Peloponnese, and cooks mainly with seasonal products from the region – she also prepares vegetarian dishes. If she has time, the bubbly proprietor likes to talk about the country and its people. *Daily, in the evening, Sun–Fri, also at lunchtime | On the main road to Afiónas | Moderate*

DIONYSOS 🌿

A taverna with a panoramic terrace high above Ágios Geórgios bay. Very friendly service. *Bekrí mezé* (a kind of Greek stew) and roast pork in wine sauce are the specialities of the house. *Daily | Afiónas | 100 m from the village square (signposted, although it cannot be reached by car) | Budget*

PÉRGOLA

The best taverna in town, many local regulars. Here, you can still go into the kitchen and take a look in the pots. *Daily | Afiónas | At the top of the main street | Budget*

SHOPPING

INSIDER TIP ▶ OLIVES AND MORE 🕐

This is where you can find first-class olive oil and products made of it, as well as creations conjured up by the owners themselves. They produce red-wine vinegar and olive paste, preserve olives and fill olive oil into tins you can take with you on the plane. If you like, you can even get it straight from the barrel. *Sun–Fri 10am–2pm and 3–9pm, Sat only 3–9pm | Afiónas | At the top end of the village square*

ESOTERIC CENTRES

Many centres offer courses, seminars and workshops throughout the six summer months. At the *Ouranos Centre* the focus is on meditation and creative programmes, while the more international *Alexis* Zorbas Centre (www.alexiszorbas.com) stresses body work. The ● *Corfu Meditation House* in Afiónas offers the right ambience for meditating with an experienced Reiki expert and two rooms.

ÁGIOS GEÓRGIOS, AFIÓNAS & ARILLÁS

ÍLIOS CENTRE ●

The perfect place for the romantically minded and shell collectors. The jewellery designer Alex in Ágios Geórgios Pagón can cast miniature olive pits, things you have found or that have been washed up on the shore, in bronze, silver or gold for you to wear as a pendant in less than 40 minutes. *Pági | On the road to the beach | www.ilios-living-art.com*

BEACHES

The sand beach at Arillás is more than 2.5 km (1.6 mi) long. The south half is in front of the town and the northern section, where you can bathe without a swimsuit, is under the cliffs on the coast. There is a third, smaller, beach to the south, 15 minutes walk from Afíonas.

ENTERTAINMENT

There are discos and music clubs in Ágios Geórgios and Arillás – but they come and go and the names change every year.

LOW BUDGET

▶ Live economically: the 10 apartments at *Harry's Bar* in Acharávi **(127 D1) (*∅ C2)* are simple but spacious. *Tel. 26 63 06 30 38, mobile 69 74 91 66 37 | Studios from 25 euros | www.harrysbar-apartments.com*

▶ A cheap swim: there are reduced prices in the *Hydropolis* fun pool near Acharávi **(127 D1) (*∅ C2)* after 3.30pm. Adults only pay 10 euros and children (5–12 years) 6 euros *(address see p. 197).*

WHERE TO STAY

INSIDER TIP PANORAMA ☼

Four apartments accommodating 2–4, on the slope below the taverna of the same name with a wonderful view of the sea and sunset are available to rent. *On the main street in Afíonas | tel. 26 63 05 18 46 | www.panoramacorfu.com | Budget*

PÓRTO TIMIÓNI ☼

Rooms and studios in a magnificent panoramic location high above the bay of Ágios Geórgios; perfect peace with absolutely no traffic noise. The ideal place to unwind and forget the rest of the world. *8 rooms | Afíonas | tel. 26 63 05 20 51 | Moderate*

WHERE TO GO

ÁGIOS STÉFANOS AVLIOTÓN
(126 A2) (*∅ A3)*

This is an unplanned conglomeration of nondescript guesthouses, summer houses, tavernas and shops but the beach with its fine sand is 2 km (1.2 mi) long. Excursion boats leave from here for the islands Mathráki and Othoní. The surfing crowd is attracted by the frequently strong winds that blow across the bay. Nudists get together in the northern section of the beach under the steep cliffs. The glass artist Perdita Mouzakiti makes objects out of coloured glass in the centre of the settlement and her sister, Claudia, is usually around to advise customers and take care of sales *(www.perditasglassart.com)*. *1000 m from Arillás, 3 km (1.9 mi) from Ágios Geórgios*

CAPE DRÁSTIS ★ ☼
(126 A1) (*∅ A–B 2)*

Of all of Corfu's beautiful coastal landscapes, the one at the far northwest tip of the island is perhaps the nicest. It can be reached after a walk of around 30 minutes along a track that is also open to cars. It begins at the primary school in Peruládes (signposted). There is initially a slight incline after which it runs down to the sea and then, all of a sudden, you have the picture-book panorama of the bay in front of you. Below the almost 100 m (330 ft) high cape, sandstone formations

PERULÁDES (126 A2) (*ω A2*)

The most north-western village on Corfu (pop. 780) has a fascinating beach. It is long and narrow and stretches along both sides of the village under a steep, towering coastline; a tarmac footpath leads down to it from the *Panórama* Bar and Restaurant *(daily | Budget)*. If you don't care for the music there, the neighbouring

Cape Drástis– the steep cliffs in the northwest can only be reached on foot or by boat

like dragons' combs surround a small bay with a little island that looks like a shark's fin in front of it. The path winds past the cape to the east and ends up in a tiny bay framed by slabs of rock. If the sea is calm, you can jump into the water here and enjoy a swim in the crystal-clear sea with a view of the steep, light-coloured cliffs that tower up right out of the water. *10 km (6.2 mi) from Arillás*

taverna *Sunset* might be more to your liking; it also has rooms in the village *(daily | Moderate)*.

There is only one – extremely elegant – hotel in Peruládes. The young brother and sister duo Aléxandros and Lukía run the 200-year-old INSIDER TIP ▶ *Villa de Loulia* with its pool and garden. *(9 rooms | tel. 26 63 09 53 94 | www.villadeloulia.gr | Expensive). 8 km (5 mi) from Arillás*

BARBÁTI & NISSÁKI

(127 E3) *(⌖ D3)* **Although, officially, the two villages on the south slope of Pantokrátor only have a tiny population of around 150 people each, they are quite built-up. Particularly the slopes of Barbáti are covered with rows of villas and flats.**

Here, the hotels are located between the road around the island and the steep rock walls of the Pantokrátor massif, while in Nissáki they can be found between the road and rocky shore. There are a few tavernas with beautiful panoramic terraces and a handful of shops along the road.

FOOD & DRINK

MÍTSOS ☙

In this simple tavern on a terrace jutting out over the sea between Nissáki's miniature beach and port, you will find one of the best lemon tarts. The location makes up for the very average pizzas, pasta and other dishes. *Daily | Above the tiny car park at the harbourside in Nissáki | Budget*

SPORT & BEACHES

Barbáti's rocky and pebbly beach is around 800 m long and up to 20 m wide. The increase in building activity on the slopes has made it rather crowded. Most of the coast near Nissáki is rocky with tiny shingle beaches and less activity. In summer, there are two water-sport centres in Barbáti and one in Nissáki on the sand-and-pebble beach below the Hotel Sol Nissáki Beach which offer a good range of activities and have equipment for hire.

WHERE TO STAY

INSIDER TIP LITTLE FARMHOUSE ☺ ●

If you want to live really rustically, Anna Polychromiádou will take care of you. The organic farmer has a holiday house for 2–4 to rent, with a donkey for the children, chickens for your breakfast egg and a lot of tales to tell about the island. *Signpost at the south entrance to the village of Kéndroma, about 100 m above the road around the island | tel. 26 63 09 12 20 | www.guestinn.com | Budget*

LA SERENISSIMA ☙

The historian Hannelore Stammler has turned a Venetian country house, painted dusky pink in the style of the island, into an elegant hotel with pool and panoramic views where lunch and dinner are provided for guests if they request it. *Above the road from Pirgí to Barbáti | tel. 26 61 09 39 22 | www.residenz-serenissima.de (click Union Jack for English text) | Expensive*

SIGHTSEEING

INSIDER TIP PALÉO CHORIÓ
(127 E3) *(⌖ D3)*

Paléo Chorió is a ghost village in which only one house has been restored since 2000. All the others are roofless ruins. The last inhabitants probably moved away before World War II. Remnants of frescoes can be found in the empty old village church, including a lovely depiction of the Twelve Apostles. You can only reach Paléo Chorió on foot, by off-road motorbike, mountain bike or 4×4; the dusty track between Vinglatúri and Pantokrátor is impassable for normal cars. *7 km (4.3 mi) from Nissáki*

PANTOKRÁTOR ☙ **(127 E2)** *(⌖ D3)*

A tarmac road leads up to Corfu's highest mountain with an altitude of around

910 m. The view from the peak is breathtaking and, if the weather is clear, reaches far into Albania and the Greek mainland. A former monastery from the 17th century located on the peak is surrounded by civil and military radio masts. Since 1998, it has been occupied once again in the summer months – alternately by a priest from a nearby mountain village and a monk from a Corfiot monastery. Since then, time-consuming restoration of the church frescoes has taken place and some of them have now regained their seventeenth-century splendour. Depictions of Jesus' descent into Hades, the Annunciation, the Nativity and Jesus in the Temple can be made out in the southern section of the vault. *Accessible during day-light hours | Entrance free | 26 km (16.2 mi) from Nissáki*

STRINÍLAS
(127 D2–3) (*𝄐 C3*)

Corfu's highest mountain village is located 630 m above sea level and has only 45 inhabitants. A taverna under the old elm on the village square offers good food. *20 km (12 mi) from Nissáki*

KASSIÓPI

(127 E1–2) (*𝄐 D2*) **The large village (pop. 1000) in the northeast of the island boasts two picturesque bays facing the Albanian coast.**

This taverna in Strinílas, Corfu's highest mountain village, is very popular

KASSIÓPI

The eastern bay is a protected natural harbour for fishing and excursion boats and yachts; most of the village's bars and taverns are located around the harbour basin. A headland with old olive trees and the overgrown ruins of a Venetian castle separates the two bays.

In Roman times, Kassiópi was a harbour town where ships stopped over to wait for better weather before sailing from Greece to Italy – taking Emperor Nero or Cicero the statesman with them.

SIGHTSEEING

CASTLE

Over the past few years, the EU has invested millions in the castle that the Venetians built in 1386 on top of the remains of old walls. The interior, completely overgrown by scrub, is illuminated at night and a sprinkler system ensures its protection from fire. The gatehouse has been restored and improvements made to the outer walls with their 13 towers. However, there was no money left to signpost the way to the castle and completely pave the path. *Free access | The path to the castle begins on the main road to the harbour opposite Panagía Kassiópitra Church.*

PANAGÍA KASSIÓPITRA CHURCH

This church from 1590 occupies the site on which the Romans had built a temple to the father of the Gods Jupiter 1600 years before. The walls of the house of worship were decorated with frescoes in the 17th century but only a few remnants have been preserved. An icon of Saint Mary from 1670 is especially beautiful. It shows the Virgin holding the baby Jesus seated on a throne with the church and castle of Kassiópi below. *Open sporadically | Access from the main road to the harbour and the terrace of the Three Brothers Tavern at the harbour*

Fishing boats as well as lots of yachts anchor in the harbour in Kassiópi

The beach in Batería may not be very long, but it's lovely

FOOD & DRINK

JÁNIS

Many varieties of English breakfast are served in this taverna on the main beach until 3pm. Most of the other dishes on the menu are also British. *Daily | Where the one-way road from the harbour meets the circular island road | Expensive*

PÓRTO ✂

The view from this harbour tavern is lovely – if tourist coaches do not happen to be in the way. The choice of dishes is extensive – the quality, average. *Galéos bourdéto* is one of the specialities of the house. *Daily | At the harbourside | Moderate*

BEACHES

The long sandy *Main Beach* skirts Kassiópi's western bay. The promenade that leads around the peninsula with the castle is about a 20-minute walk and provides access to tiny shingle beaches. The most beautiful beach in Kassiópi, *Batería Beach*,

at the head of the peninsula, is only about 80 m long; deckchairs and umbrellas are available for hire. It is also possible to swim from the rocks to the east of the harbour.

ENTERTAINMENT

The best way to spend the evening is in one of the bars at the harbour. The *Passion Disco* on the south side of the basin opens its doors at midnight, with a British DJ usually playing the latest hits.

WHERE TO STAY

Most of the rooms in Kassiópi are in the hands of British and Scandinavian tourist agencies and not available to individual travellers. Other renters only accept guests who stay for more than one night.

OÁSIS

The small hotel above the taverna of the same name, founded in 1935, is a godsend to those who only want to spend one night in Kassiópi. If you choose a room without a view, on the mountain side, you will even have a peaceful night. Private car park behind the house. The proprietor Lóla Sarakinú's daughter, Mandi, speaks English. *30 rooms | Odós Kassiopítras 6 | Main road to the harbour | Budget*

ARAKINOÚ ROOMS

An old-fashioned guesthouse with very reasonable prices and many regular guests. The four rooms and studios are located around a small courtyard above a row of shops virtually on the harbour. The owner, Helena, takes good care of her guests. *On the main road opposite the entrance to the churchyard. | tel. 26 63 08 12 31 | Budget*

SIGHTSEEING

ÁGIOS STÉFANOS SINIÉS
(127 F2) (*∅ E3*)

Ágios Stefános Siniés (pop. 230) is the closest Corfiot village to Albania. Yachtsmen anchor in the long bay and several tavernas on the shore do all they can to attract guests. There are a few private rooms, but most are reserved for British tourist agencies. You can rent a motorboat for a tour along the coast. *6 km (3.7 mi) from Kassiópi*

AGNÍ (127 E–F3) (*∅ D–E 3*)

Agní is a peaceful bay with a 150 m-long, white shingle-and-stone beach, a few private rooms and three tavernas. Wooden jetties where yachts moor jut out into the water. The three inns all serve good fresh fish. There are many dishes for vegetarians on the menu of the *Agní* tavern – *marída jemistá*, sardines filled with cheese, garlic and parsley, are quite innovative. Scampi pilaf, *piláfi me gárides*, is the hit in *Toula's Taverna (all open daily | Budget)*. You should use the car park on

the outskirts of the village; it is often impossible to turn at the waterside! *11 km (6.8 mi) from Kassiópi*

AVLÁKI (127 F2) (*∅ E2*)

The 500 m-long shingle beach to the southeast of Kassiópi is still hardly built up. There is only one taverna, a watersport centre and the modern apartment-hotel Bella Mare *(27 rooms | tel.: 26 63 08 19 97 | Expensive)*. You can walk there from Kassiópi in around 25 minutes. *2 km (1.2 mi) from Kassiópi*

KALÁMI
(127 F3) (*∅ E3*)

The tiny hamlet of Kalámi on the coast is almost smothered by a large holiday club complex. A visit can be recommended for fans of Lawrence Durrell's Corfu classic *Prospero's Cell*. The Durrell family lived in Kalámi in the 1930s – in the large property on the shore called *White House*. The four-bedroomed building can be rented as a

Paleokastrítsa and the adjoining coastal areas are among the most beautiful on Corfu

holiday house; the Durrell family's dining table is still there! *(www.white-house-corfu. gr | Budget)*. There is now a good taverna on the ground floor *(daily | Budget)*
The 250 m-long pebble-and-stone beach is relatively small for so many summer holidaymakers. However, there is a track from here to *Gialiskári Beach* in the north where there are a lot less people on the pebbly beach and rocks. This is also an interesting underwater world for snorkelers. *11 km (6.8 mi) from Kassiópi*

KAMINÁKI BEACH
(127 E3) (Ø D3)
The much-photographed shingle beach, measuring just 100 × 15 m, lies in front of a tiny coastal settlement with two tavernas *(Budget)* and a water-sport business *(www.kaminakiboats.com)* that also rents out motorboats without a skipper. There are around 60 loungers under 30 sunshades on the beach, but there is always enough space for your towel if you prefer.

KULÚRA (127 F3) (Ø E3)
The semi-oval harbour basin in front of the fortified country seat from the 16th century in Kulúra is one of Corfu's standard postcard images. It is worth taking a photo but a waste of time driving down to the harbour where there are hardly any parking spaces. The house has belonged to an Italian family since 1986 and is off-limits to holidaymakers. *10 km (6.2 mi) from Kassiópi*

PALEO-KASTRÍTSA, LÁKONES & LIAPÁDES

(126 B–C4) (Ø B4) **Paleokastrítsa, which actually forms part of the mountain village of Lákones, and the coastal**

settlement of another mountain village, Liapádes, both lie in a large bay.

It is separated into a series of smaller bays by several rocky headlands. The coast is mainly stony, but there are some small sandy beaches – many of which can only be reached by boat. The lush green stretches all the way down to the water's edge and slopes rise up several hundred metres into the hinterland.

Many Corfiots consider *Paleokastrítsa* the most beautiful spot on earth. There is no village centre as such, the hotels, houses and tavernas being loosely scattered in a magnificent landscape and are often hidden between olive groves and cypresses. You will need to walk for about 3.5 km (2.2 mi) if you want to see all of Paleokastrítsa.

The most beautiful view of the bay is from the large ☼ mountain village of *Lákones* that is also called the 'balcony of the Ionian Sea'. Most of the cafés and restaurants have generous terraces offering panoramic views. A 40-minute INSIDER**TIP** walk along a path through an olive grove will take you down to Paleokastrítsa; the serpentine road is about 6 km (3.7 mi) long.

Liapádes on the other hand is around 1000 m from the coast and has no view of the sea. A holiday settlement stretches from the old village to Liapádes Beach on the bay. The small village square is really charming, being bordered by the terraces of five traditional cafés and the bell tower of the village church. The farmers still make their way across the square with their donkeys.

SIGHTSEEING

PANAGÍA THEOTÓKU TIS PALEO-KASTRÍTSAS MONASTERY ★ ☼

The white monastery of the 'The Holy Bearer of God of Paleokastrítsa' perches high above the sea on a steep cliff at the end of the bay. With its magnificent view, shady arcades, courtyard full of flowers

Tourist magnet: the romantic monastery Panágia Theotóku tis Paleokastrítsas

and beautiful church, it is one of the major and most-visited attractions on Corfu. Three monks still live here accompanied by several elderly and handicapped people who spend their summer holidays with them.

The monastery was founded in the 12th century; however the present building was erected in the 18th. You can see God the Father, the Son and the Holy Ghost in the form of a white dove painted on the ceiling of the single-nave church. The church's most precious icon has been placed at the front on the left-hand wall. The work only measures 43 × 33 cm and shows three Fathers of the Church identifiable by their stoles decorated with crosses. Behind them, there is a depiction of a dramatic event that actually occurred in Corfu on the feast day of these three saints, on 30 January, in 1653. A firework that had been lit in their honour exploded while a nurse holding a child in her arms was standing nearby. As if by miracle, the child remained uninjured although the nurse was killed. She can be seen clearly in the right-hand section of the painting. Blood is pouring out of her side, she falls to the ground while still holding the child in her arms. The child's parents donated the icon as a sign of their gratitude to the saints for this (modest) miracle; the text to the right of the strip of pictures gives a detailed description of the occurrence.

There are two other icons at the back of the church on the left-hand and right-hand walls. They were painted in 1713 and illustrate four scenes of the Creation. *April–Oct daily 7am–1pm and 3–8pm; the best time to visit is before 9am and after 5pm when the hordes of tourists have left the church. Whatever you do, don't park in the spaces reserved for buses – the drivers will block you in mercilessly! | Entrance free*

FOOD & DRINK

CASTELINO ♉

Not only can you look down onto Paleokastrítsa Bay from the highest restaurant in the region, you can also see all the way to Kérkyra and the Greek mainland. The proprietors Spíros and Frósso Chalíkia serve what is probably the island's best walnut cake *(karidópitta)* and many other homemade Corfiot specialities on the several floors of their restaurant. *Daily | Above the road from Lákones to Makrádes, park on the road | Expensive*

HORIZON ♉

Taverna with a lovely panoramic terrace and very friendly service. If you ask, you can have boiled potatoes as a side dish instead of the omnipresent chips. *Daily | On the main road, next to Hotel Odysseus | Moderate*

SHOPPING

ÁLKIS ☺

Since 1986 Mr Alkibíade has passionately devoted himself to his search for beautifully grained olive wood to create unique objects after his own designs. He is considered the most gifted olive-wood carver on the island. *Lákones | On the left as you exit the village on the road to Mákrades*

STREET MARKET

During the tourist season, the top end of the road to Panagía Theotóku ti Paleokastrítsas Monastery and the square in front of it turn into a large street market every morning at around 10am when Africans sell arts and crafts from their native countries and Corfiots painted objects of all sorts. The stones painted with Corfiot motifs by Ilía Sigouroú make nice little gifts and only cost from 3 euros upwards. She will sign them on the back if you want and can usually be found on the tiny lookout platform in front of the church opposite the café (*Moderate*) from whose terrace you have a wonderful view of the steep coastline and Angelókastro Castle.

BEACHES

The pebble beaches in the three large bays *Ambeláki*, *Spíridon* and *Alípa* are easy to reach. Flights of steps lead from the main road down to other smaller pebbly bays. *Liapádes'* shingle beach is around 150 km (9.3 mi) long. None of them are really ideal for children. Boat taxis leave from *Spíridon Beach*, the pier in front of the La Grotta Bar, the harbour at *Alípa Beach* and *Liapádes Beach* for the numerous other sandy and shingle bays that can only be reached from the sea. If you wish, you can rent a motorboat with up to 30 HP – and you don't need a licence.

ENTERTAINMENT

142 steps lead from the main road opposite Hotel Paleokastrítsa to a small bar in an artificial grotto made of volcanic rock. Here, you can listen to the owner's favourite music or soak up the sound of the sea. *Daily | Paleokastrítsa*

WHERE TO STAY

AKROTIRI BEACH ꭗ
This five-storey hotel – with its freshwater swimming pool high above one of the many lovely bays in Paleokastrítsa – can be seen from afar. The small shingle beach with water-sport facilities can be reached via a small flight of steps. *127 rooms | On the main road | tel. 26 63 04 12 75 | www.akotriri-beach.com | Expensive*

GOLDEN FOX ★
For motorised holidaymakers who don't necessarily want to stay near the beach, there is probably no lovelier accommodation in northern Corfu than *Golden Fox's* six studios. Four of them have a ꭗ balcony with a view of the sea, as well as the bays in Paleokastrítsa and Angelókastro Castle. The complex high above the sea also has a good restaurant, a bar, a large souvenir shop and a beautifully designed freshwater pool. Unfortunately, however, the rooms are only simply equipped. *11 studios | On the road from Lákones to Makrádes | tel. 26 63 04 91 01 | www.corfugoldenfox.com | Moderate–Expensive*

LIAPÁDES BEACH
100 m from the beach and 1500 m from the centre of the village, with pool and a very good hotel restaurant. *50 rooms | On the road to the beach | tel. 26 63 04 12 94 | Budget*

INSIDER TIP VILLA FIORITA STUDIOS
Guesthouse with a large garden run by the friendly Loúlis family. 100 m from the sea, two minutes from a bus stop. *15 studios away from the main road in the village | tel. 26 63 04 13 52 | fiorita@shms. gr | Moderate*

WHERE TO GO

ANGELÓKASTRO ★ ꭗ
(126 B4) (ɯ B4)
The ruins of this Byzantine-Venetian 'Angels' Castle' stand high above the west coast on a mountain peak with steep slopes on all sides. Until the last Turkish invasion of the island in 1716, this repeatedly offered refuge to the population of northern Corfu when enemies or pirates approached. Nobody was ever able to conquer Angelókastro. A tarmac road leads

Perfectly built on the top of a cliff: Angelókastro Castle

from Makrádes to a car park 700 metres beyond Kriní at the foot of the castle hill. You'll have to walk up a steep path for the last 7 to 10 minutes but you will be rewarded with a wonderful view for your effort. *Tue–Sun 8am–3pm | Entrance free | 5.5 km (3.4 mi) from Lákones*

MAKRÁDES (126 B4) (*Ø B4*)

Makrádes (pop. 300) is a large mountain village with many old houses and narrow lanes. Nowhere else on Corfu have so many inhabitants specialised in selling herbs and local table wine as here. Fierce competition forces them to make furious attempts to stop any passing car! In the Colombo Taverna *(daily | Budget)* on the village square there is a more than 200-year-old olive press and you can sample many Corfiot specialities and all kinds of meat from the charcoal grill. *3 km (1.9 mi) from Lákones*

VÍSTONAS
(126 B4) (*Ø B4*)

The mountain village (population 160) itself, on the road from Makrádes to the Trumbétta Pass and located in the midst of olive groves, has little of interest as such.

However, the most delightful wine stand on the island can be found not far away on the road to Pági ☺ **INSIDER TIP** *To Chelidóni* – which means 'the swallow'. Panajótis Koríkis and his wife can be found here every day from 10am onwards at their picturesque tables – set with loving care – opposite their vineyards. They will let you taste their semi-sweet red and fruity dry white table wine before you buy it; they also sell local walnuts, as well as olive oil and herbs at reasonable prices. *6 km (3.7 mi) from Lákones, turn left at the sign on the outskirts of the village.*

THE SOUTH

Hills covered with olive groves stretch across most of the area between Ágios Górdis, Benítses and Cape Asprókavos on Corfu. And, the west coast in particular is lined with miles of sandy beaches.

Lake Koríssion, the largest on the island, and the former salt-works near Lefkími are unique landscapes with a character of their very own. There is also an unusual sight between the two seaside resorts of Messongí and Moraítika, as well as in Lefkími, where fishing boats are not moored directly along the coast but in romantic river harbours. The south of the island, however, does not have many historical sights to offer. This is the place to enjoy the great outdoors and the pris-

tine state of many villages and beaches. The holiday centres at Messongí and Moraítika are the only areas affected by mass tourism. Once you are away from them, you will find many tranquil coastal towns and villages dotted along Corfu's south coast.

ÁGIOS GEÓRGIOS ARGIRÁDON

(128 B–C 4–5) (𝟙 E8) Seven kilometres (4.3 mi) of sandy beach – without any

Corfu's gentler side: olive groves, beaches that are easy to reach, Lake Koríssion and many peaceful coastal towns

shade and still undiscovered by deckchair and umbrella hawkers – can be found between Ágios Geórgios Argirádon, which is also known as Ágios Geórgios South, (pop. 500) and the few houses in Chalikúnas. Fringed by high dunes, it is a little bit like a beach on the North Sea in Denmark.

You will not see wooded mountains behind the beach as you do elsewhere on Corfu but a steppe-like coastal plain with the large Lake Koríssion that is rich in eels. Ágios Geórgios itself is a holiday resort stretching along the coast for almost 3 km (1.9 mi) but without any real centre. The neighbouring village of Chalikúnas is made up of a few guest-houses and three tavernas. Those seeking peace and quiet will feel at home in Chalikúnas, while those who want at least a little entertainment and nightlife will prefer Ágios Geórgios.

Only a small strip of land separates Lake Koríssion from the sea

SIGHTSEEING

LAKE KORÍSSION ★
(128 B–C4) (*D8*)

The lake is 5 km (3.1 mi) long and up to 1000 m wide and is separated from the sea by a strip of sand and dunes but connected to it by a narrow, natural channel. Depending on the tides and direction of the wind, water either flows into the lake or back into the sea. This keeps the lake clean and attracts many fish. The channel is crossed by a bridge making tours around the lake by mountainbike or on foot possible.

FOOD & DRINK

ALONÁKI ★ ●

You will feel like you are in the Garden of Eden when you sit in this idyllic taverna above the small bay with its sandy beach to the north of the long dune beach at Chalikúnas. A myna bird chatters and laughs in its aviary, cats vie for your attention and swallows nest under the wooden roof of the terrace. Apricots and figs fall almost directly into your mouth. The innkeeper's family serves delicacies including rabbit *stifádo*, *skórpios bourdéto* and stuffed cabbage leaves – *lachanodolmádes*. *Daily | Well signposted, on the road to Chalikúnas beach | Budget*

INSIDER TIP O KAFÉSAS ☼

In the most unusual taverna in Ágios Geórgios, you sit on terraces above a little-used road with a view of the sea. Ákis the proprietor and his wife from New Zealand, Miriam, have decorated the taverna tastefully. The bread comes straight out of the clay oven; the vegetables, olive oil and chickens are from their farm and they even smoke the fish themselves. The mixed pickles – *toursí* – are in a league of their own and the *bourdéto* is made with stingray. There is usually live Greek music on Saturday evening. *Daily | On the coast road, to the south of the village | Moderate*

BEACHES

In addition to the 7 km (4.3 mi) *Chalikúnas Beach*, you can also bathe on the narrow sandy beach that runs along the entire south half of Ágios Geórgios Argirádon beneath the low but steep coastline. A sandy beach of around 200 m continues to the north of the main beach at Chalikúnas below Pension Alonáki. This is not only a meeting place for good surfers but also kite surfers as the only kite-surf facility on Corfu is in *Café Harley*.

ENTERTAINMENT

HARLEY

This cafe is open all day and develops into a lively meeting place for surfers in the evening. This is where they not only talk shop and listen to good music but also play *távli* and 'KoJa' golf – a natural kind of miniature golf developed by the owners. *Daily | At the north end of the coast road*

MANGO BAR 🌿

Comfy sofas in colourful surroundings invite you to chill-out with cocktails and a sea view in the evening. *Daily | At the north end of the coast road*

WHERE TO STAY

INSIDER TIP ALONÁKI

The proprietor, who speaks English, rents 15 rooms and apartments above her tavern of the same name and in the building next door. This is the only place where you can try the small, crisply fried, crabs from Lake Koríssion. Not the normal taverna fare but Corfiot cuisine just like the cook would serve her guests at home. *Tel. 26 61 07 58 72; in winter 26 62 07 61 19 | Budget*

GOLDEN SANDS

Two-storey hotel with a large pool area on the coast road in the southern part of Ágios Geórgios. Laid-back atmosphere, spacious balconies; guests who want to spend just one night are also welcome. *78 rooms | tel. 26 62 05 12 25 | Budget*

MARIN-CHRISTEL

Small, charming and well-looked-after apartment complex owned by a Greek doctor; absolute peace and quiet but without any shade. Approx. 10 minutes walk to the beach. *7 apartments | tel. 26 62 07 59 47 | Moderate*

INSIDER TIP Livadiótis *Winery (daily 10am–2pm)*. The owner, Sotíris Livadiótis, is a passionate winegrower who only produces around 20,000 bottles of dry red

Lefkími: boats moored side by side in the little riverside harbour

WHERE TO GO

GARDÍKI
(128 B4) *(ØD 7–8)*
The 13th-century Byzantine castle (free access), with its octagonal defence wall and towers of quarried stone with rows of brick, is the most important historical site in the southern part of the island. You can clamber around its (unsecured) walls. Concert and theatre performances are held here in July.
When you travel on to Lake Koríssion, past fields of flowers, you will come to

and white wine every year. Of course, you can taste the wine and visit the cellars. These have not been spruced up for visitors but have kept their very rural, very Greek and somewhat unkempt, natural character. *13 km (8.1mi) from Ágios Geórgios*

KÁVOS
(129 F5–6) *(ØG9)*
Every year, the most southerly town on Corfu (pop. 850) is pounced upon by the Greek press and private television. Together with Faliráki on Rhodes and Mália on Crete, Kávos, with its mainly young

tourists, forms what the Greeks consider an 'unholy' trinity. Those who are less discrete, simply describe Kávos as the 'British party mile'. You will not find much relaxation here but any number of clubs, restaurants and bars. *22 km (13.7 mi) from Ágios Geórgios | English website: www.kavos.biz*

LEFKÍMI
(129 E5) *(ﬧ F8)*
The River Chimarós flows through Lefkími – with a population of 3500, the largest town in the south. It is wide and deep enough to be used by the small sport and fishing boats that are anchored in the centre of the village. Starting at the bridge over the river, a road runs along the right bank to the sandy beach at Lefkími that is mainly used by the locals. The only taverna in this town that is still almost untouched by tourism is located near the bridge. The former saltworks at Alýkes on a bay with a narrow sandy beach is also part of Lefkími. The shore here is extremely flat and even small children can swim far out and still be able to touch the bottom. *16 km (9.9 mi) from Ágios Geórgios*

MARATHIÁS
(129 D5) *(ﬧ F8)*
Small inland village with a cul-de-sac leading down to the beach of the same name. It is miles long and its fine sand shimmers a light red in the sun. *9 km (5.6 mi) from Ágios Geórgios*

PERIVÓLI
(129 D5) *(ﬧ F8)*
You can reach the coastal hamlet of *Ágia Varvára*, known locally as Santa Barbara, from this large inland village (pop. 1400). The sandy beach is more than 1000 m long and joins up with the next beach at Marathiás. Apartments and holiday homes for rent. *13 km (8.1 mi) from Ágios Geórgios*

VITALÁDES (129 D5) *(ﬧ E8)*
A dead-end leads from Vitaládes to the young seaside resort of INSIDER TIP *Gardénos* with its peaceful beach of fine sand, two tavernas and several guesthouses including the *Spíti Xifías (8 rooms | tel. 26 62 02 43 74 | Budget)*. Signposts will point you in the direction of the *'Virgin Beaches' Pérka* and *Megáli Lakiá*. From *Gardénos Beach* there is a fine view of Páxos Island. *14 km (8.7 mi) from Ágios Geórgios*

ÁGIOS GÓRDIS

(128 B2) *(ﬧ D6)* **High mountain slopes with striking rock formations soar up from both ends of the long, sandy beach at Ágios Górdis (also known as Ágios Górdios).**

LOW BUDGET

▶ ● Pools for all: many small hotels and apartment complexes, such as Pension Égrypos in Petríti **(129 D4)** *(ﬧ E8)*, Hotel Golden Sands in Ágios Geórgios Argirádon **(128 C5)** *(ﬧ E8)* and Hotel Romantic View in Ágios Górdis **(128 B2)** *(ﬧ D6)*, also welcome guests who are not staying there but have something to eat or drink at the pool, which they can then use free of charge.

▶ Cheap trips to the mainland: the ferries from Lefkími **(129 E5)** *(ﬧ F8)* to Igoumenítsa are cheaper than those departing from Corfu Town. You save around 2.50 euros per person and 9 euros per car for a single crossing.

ÁGIOS GÓRDIS

Sandy beach below the towering cliffs: Ágios Górdis

The bay is bordered to the south by a rocky pinnacle, the *Orthólithos*, rising out of the water. This gives Ágios Górdis its unique atmosphere. The village is only a tourist resort in summer and in autumn its inhabitants move back up to their native villages of *Káto Garúna* and *Sinarádes*. Most of the tavernas and shops are located on the 120 m-long main road to the beach.

FOOD & DRINK

LINDA'S
The owner and cook Frideriki serves her guests good, home-style Greek cooking. *Daily, evenings only | On the main road to the beach | Moderate*

THÁLASSA
Family-run, beach taverna with pizza from a stone oven and many homemade dishes. Friendly service by the owner. *Daily | On the beach | Budget*

ENTERTAINMENT

ARK BEACH CAFÉ
The most stylish beach bar in town. Sun beds during the day; chill out at sunset. *Daily from 9am | Southern beach section*

MIKE'S DANCING PUB
The place where young holidaymakers in the village meet late in the evening. *Daily from 6pm | At the junction bus stop*

WHERE TO STAY

DANDÍDIS
Studios and apartments, especially suitable for small children, in a house on the beach. *14 rooms | Middle beach section | tel. 26 61 05 32 32 | www.dandidis.com | Moderate*

ROMANTIC VIEW ☼
The rooms are different in size and price, but most have a balcony with a sea view; there is a large terrace with a pool, whirlpool, paddling pool and an open-air restaurant (not only for hotel guests). 10 min walk downhill – 15 min uphill – from the beach. *80 rooms | On the road to Sinarádes | tel. 26 61 05 43 51 | Moderate*

SENSIMAR AGIOS GORDIOS

What makes this hotel so unique is its breathtaking location between the rocks on the coast and the bizarre pinnacle of stone behind the complex. The sand-and-pebble beach is short and narrow – there is in fact more room around the pool – but it is only a brief walk to the long beach in the village. Quite large rooms (21–23 m²). Taken over by the Sensimar Group in 2009, the hotel is run on an obligatory, all-inclusive policy. The hotel does not accept bookings for under 18-year-olds – even in the company of their parents. *264 rooms | Can only be booked through a travel agent | www.sensimar.com | Expensive*

WHERE TO GO

ÁGIOS MATTHEÓS (128 B3) (*ᗠ D7*)

The large mountain village (pop. 1450) is located in an especially fertile high-lying valley without a view of the sea. Most of its inhabitants live from olive cultivation. A track, that is only suitable for 4×4s, leads up to *Pantokrátoras Monastery* – that is no longer used – 5 km (3.1 mi) away. *10 km (6.2 mi) from Ágios Górdis*

PARAMÓNAS ★ (128 B3) (*ᗠ D7*)

This coastal settlement, with only a few houses and a 300 m-long sand-and-shingle beach, is part of the parish of Ágios Mattheós. People looking for peace and quiet stay in Sunset Pension with its friendly service *(6 rooms | tel. 26 61 07 51 49 | Budget)* or *Paramónas Hotel (22 rooms | tel. 26 61 07 56 95 | www.paramonas-hotel.de | Moderate).* **INSIDER TIP** The modern *Skála* has one of the most beautiful gardens on the island and a small pool *(10 rooms | tel. 26 61 07 50 32 and 26 61 07 51 08 | Moderate). Plóri* Restaurant is located directly on the beach about 80 m from this guesthouse and 100 m to the south of Sunset *(daily | Budget). 13 km (8.1 mi) from Ágios Górdis*

PENDÁTI ☀ (128 A–B2) (*ᗠ C–D 6*)

If you stay in Ágios Górdis, you should take the 20–30 minute walk up to the unspoiled mountain village of Pendáti (pop. 500) at least once. The ☀ **INSIDER TIP** view from *Chris' Place* Snackbar is breathtaking and the moussaká very good. *11 km (6.8 mi) from Ágios Górdis by road; 2 km (1.2 mi) on foot.*

THE FISH CULT

The Corfiots feel that the sea is the best pantry. At home, they usually eat small, inexpensive fish but when they go out, only the best is good enough. And they always order more than they can eat. Fish is a cult object; it has religious significance as the symbol of Christ and is a healthy food. These are just two reasons that make fish farming one of the most important economic pillars on the Ionian Islands. The more than 500 Greek fish farms even deliver to restaurants and markets in Germany and Italy. Fish that are not to be found in local waters are imported from Thailand, Indonesia and South America. The scampi the Greeks love so much are just as fresh in many countries in northern Europe. If you want to try regional fish, you should limit yourself to small *gópes, gávri* and *marídes*. These are often caught by small trawlers sailing from Corfiot harbours.

MESSONGÍ-MORAÍTIKA

(128 C3–4) (⟋ D–E 7) A small river separates Messongí (pop. 290) from Moraítika (pop. 600) and flows into the sea near the bridge connecting the two villages. Fishing and excursion boats moor on both banks.

You will search in vain for anything old in the historical centre of Messongí that runs parallel to the beach. The main axis of Moraítika is formed by the busy road to the south of the island. Large hotel complexes have been built on the sea side. The houses of the old village of Moraítika and several tavernas line the slope on the land side.

FOOD & DRINK

75 STEPS ☙

Restaurant in a lush setting with a roof terrace and view of the sea and mountains. *Daily | 1800 m past the bridge on the road to Chlómos | Moderate*

MARILENA

Small, unpretentious taverna shaded by trees and run by a multi-lingual owner. Fresh, mainly regional, food and excellent value for money. *Daily, in the evening | At the southern end of Messongí Beach | www.bacchus.gr | Budget*

TÁSSOS VILLAGE GRILL ★ ☙

This modest taverna in the old centre of Moraítika has a lot of enthusiastic regular guests. Tássos, the proprietor, grills delicate lamb and juicy pork chops next to the tables on the terrace; his sons, Kóstas and Spíros (a former banker), take care of the service and chat with the guests. Their fisherman friends from the village bring their latest catch. It is a good idea to come early to avoid waiting. Excellent value for money and the view from the roof terrace reaches down to the sea. *Daily, in the evening | Moraítika | Budget*

ZAKS

Vegetarian dishes and flambé steaks are served on a flower-decked terrace. Zacharías, the owner, learned his art in England and Switzerland. *Daily, in the evening | Messongí, on the main road near the bridge | Expensive*

BEACHES

The beach in Moraítika is wider than the one in Messongí – both are mainly coarse sand and shingle. In Messongí, it is bordered by an almost endless row of small

tavernas; the bars and tavernas in Moraítika are more spread out and you will not feel that you are lying directly in front of a row of houses. However, neither village has a shore promenade. Attempts have been made to remedy this in Moraítika by creating a wooden board-walk. Excursion boats offering day tours to the island of Páxos, the rocky Greek mainland and Kérkyra depart from the harbour at the mouth of the River Messongí.

ENTERTAINMENT

VERY COCO

Disco bar with swimming pool. Excellent strawberry daiquiris, international main-stream and, occasionally, Greek music. *Daily from 9pm | Main island road*

WHERE TO STAY

INSIDER TIP CHRISTINA

This friendly modern hotel directly on the beach at Messongí is popular and usually only accepts guests who stay for at least one week. Beach freaks will like the A-category rooms: open the terrace door and you are on the beach and then straight in the water. *16 rooms | Messongí | Access from the coast road | tel. 26 61 07 67 71 | www.hotelchristina.gr | Moderate*

MESSONGÍ BEACH

Spacious, old-style hotel complex on the beach with one seawater and three fresh-water pools, three tennis courts and a diving school. Organised activities for children. *828 rooms | tel. 26 61 07 68 84 | www.messonghibeach.gr | Expensive*

Mesongí and Moraítaki have merged to make one popular holiday resort

Shark jaws and coral are on display in the small shell museum in Benítses

WHERE TO GO

ÁGII DÉKA ☙ (128 B2) (𝄞 D6)

The village of the 'Ten Saints' (pop. 180) lies high up on a mountain slope crowned by a white radar dome that can be seen from afar. A 3.5 km (2.2 mi) long track (cemented at the beginning) that 4×4s can negotiate, leads up to it. *Pantokrátoras Monastery*, now only inhabited by cats *(free access)* is located a few hundred metres away from the radar dome at the other end of the plateau in the middle of a grove of fig, walnut and cherry trees. There is a small modern chapel dedicated to the Prophet Elijah a few steps above the monastery from where there is a magnificent view of the west coast of Corfu and Lake Koríssion. *17 km (10.6 mi) from Messongí*

BENÍTSES (128 C2) (𝄞 D6)

The former fishing village is now a holiday resort (pop. 800) with too many people crowding the small beach. The car park at the harbour leaves a lot to be desired. Those interested in archaeology can visit the scant remains of the *baths of a Roman villa* from the 2nd century AD. Sections of the outer walls are 4 m high and it is still possible to recognise the pool *(free access | Signposted from the northern car park on the coast road)*.

There is a small private Shell Museum at the northern end of Benítses *(daily 10am–6pm; 8pm in July and August | Entrance 4 euros | www.corfushellmuseum.com)* that displays shells from all over the world as well as sharks' jaws and coral. The owner, Napoleon Sagías, is usually on hand to explain everything to his visitors. *8 km (5 mi) from Messongí*

BÚKARI (129 D4) (𝄞 E7)

The small fishing harbour (pop. 50) on the east coast is one of the quietest places on Corfu. It is only about a 1¾ hour walk from Messongí along the little-used coast road. The small shingle beach at Búkari slopes gently into the sea and shade is provided by tamarisk trees. Its fish tavernas make Búkari a popular destination for the Corfiots at weekends. ★ *Spíros Karidis' Fish Taverna*, directly on the harbour, is especially popular *(daily | Expensive)*.

The proprietor always has a fine selection of fresh fish and lobster on hand, cooks an excellent *bourdéto* that is almost like a fish soup, and serves wine straight from the barrel, which goes down really well. You are welcome to pick your dessert directly from the fruit trees in the garden. *6 km (3.7 mi) from Messongí*

CHLÓMOS ★ (128 C4) (*⌀ E 7–8*)

Chlómos has only 700 inhabitants and is one of the loveliest mountain villages in the south of the island. The view of its tiled roofs from ⚡ *Taxiárchis Church* at the top of the village is especially captivating. The ⚡ INSIDER TIP *Balis* Taverna near the coast on the edge of the village offers a fine view of Chlómos *(daily | Budget)*; it is also a good place for a drink. *5 km (3.1 mi) from Messongí*

PETRÍTI (129 D4) (*⌀ E8*)

Large boats frequently drop anchor at the fishing harbour of this hamlet (pop. 100) on the west coast. They are on the look out for sardines and anchovies and – as is often the case with big fishing boats in Greece – most of the crew are Egyptian from villages in the Nile Delta. Fish is still relatively inexpensive in the village tavernas. A strange rock with three crosses and the Greek and Byzantine flags lies just off the narrow beach. A former local policeman, who often sits on a self-made raft near the island and sings, erected them along with a small model of a church. This is to remind people that the small island was once the site of a church dedicated to St. Nicholas that is, today, completely in ruins. The 70 m long, sandy *Nótos Beach* lies on the other side of the rocky island at the south end of the village. An old olive grove reaches down to the shore. The food in the ● INSIDER TIP *Panórama* taverna *(Budget)* above the beach is excellent and the deckchairs on the shore can be used

free of charge. The small garden on the gentle slope between the taverna and sea is one of the loveliest on the island and you will feel like you are in a private villa by the sea. The owners, Thanássis Vagiás and his wife Ína, rent 15 spacious apartments in a tranquil house with the flair of traditional Corfiot island life about 100 m further inland *(Tel. 26 62 05 17 07 | www.panoramacorfu.gr | Budget)*.

You can live well in the *Hotel Petríti* in a small, very green, high-lying inland valley. Four two-storey buildings with tiled roofs are grouped around a pool; the hotel bus takes you to the various beaches, free of charge, several times a day. The owner's family takes great care of its guests and is happy to organise transfers to the airport. The cockcrow in the morning is another of the rural charms *(32 rooms | Between Petríti and Vasislátika | tel. 26 62 05 21 32 | www.regina-hotel.de | Moderate)*. *15 km (9.3 mi) from Messongí*

Búkari: tranquil coastal village with good fish tavernas

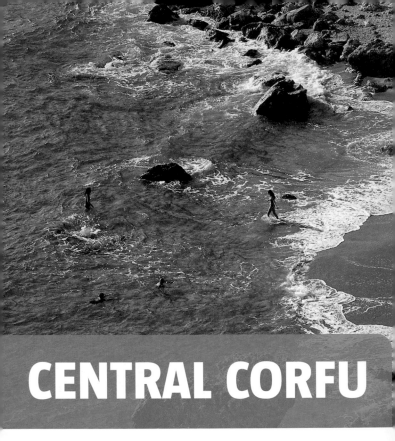

CENTRAL CORFU

Most of the island's large, luxury hotels are located in the broad bay between Kérkyra and Pantokrátor. But, only the birds see that. The massive hotel blocks that are found on other Mediterranean shores are completely missing on Corfu's coasts.

Even the larger complexes are well hidden between lush greenery, or separated from each other by gently rolling hills or coastal bays. Here, you will be able to spend your holidays in park-like surroundings on the seashore. Most of the beaches are narrow and usually pebbly, but the hotels offset this with spacious, beautiful sunbathing lawns and pool terraces. The sheltered bays are particularly attractive for water-

skiing and paragliding. The beaches slope gradually into the water and are well suited for children (with bathing shoes) and many hotels and water-sport facilities have built wooden jetties that can be used for sunbathing. If you want to take a swim, ladders make it easier to access deeper water directly.

A tourist infrastructure with tavernas, cafés, souvenir shops, supermarkets and bars has developed in those areas that only come alive in summer. But the island's capital, with its shopping and cultural opportunities, is not far away. Inexpensive buses run until late in the night and night owls can take a taxi home for a relatively low fare.

Photo: Mirtiotissa Beach

From a former hippie spot to up-market holiday area: swimming during the day and a visit to the island's capital at night

The west coast in central Corfu is completely different in character to the eastern side of the island. Lovely old villages like Pélekas – once a favourite among the hippie crowd in its day and still a popular destination for backpackers now – and Sinirádes nestle on the hills further inland and there are a number of no-through-roads that wind their way down to long, wide and very inviting sandy beaches. Hotel settlements such as Glífada and Érmones, with its good water-sport centre, diving school and (perhaps rather surprisingly) the only golf course on the Ionian Islands, as well as many other facilities, have sprung up at the ends of these beaches. There is still no tarmac road, only a gruelling dirt and cement path, down to the beach at Mirtiótis. And the only substantial building as such near the beach is a monastery – and that's at the far end of the beach which is particularly popular among nudists.

DAFNÍLA & DASSIÁ

(127 D4) (*C–D 4*) **Dafníla, on a lush, green hilly peninsula, and Dassiá to its north form Corfu's most luxurious holiday region.**

Here, the hotels are not located directly on the beach but high above the sea amid the vegetation. Parachutes float over the water, water-skiers and banana-riders

deal of local charm in the villages in the hinterland that can also be explored on horseback.

SIGHTSEEING

IPAPÁNTI CHURCH ★

Every Corfu holidaymaker is familiar with the monastery island of Vlachérna – at least, from postcards. However, its smaller, but just as lovely counterpart is largely unknown. Going across the short causeway, you will feel like you are on a large

Picturesquely surrounded by water. The small church in Ipapánti in the south of Dafníla

circle the beaches. 'Relaxing in comfort' is the motto – and this applies especially to the spa areas in the complexes. There is no use looking for historical village centres here but you can still find a great

inland lake: Guviá bay is completely enclosed by low, green hills and the opening to the sea is nowhere to be seen. In the distance, you can just make out Guviá's marina and the old shipyard buildings.

A beautiful garden with midday flowers, cacti, agaves and palm trees has been planted around the church – and there are benches where you can sit and admire them. This romantic place is especially popular for weddings. *Daily, from midday | Follow the small signpost to Koméno on the main island road*

FOOD & DRINK

ETRUSCO

Gastronomic guides describe Ettore Botrini's restaurant as the 'avant-garde of Greek gastronomy', the best restaurant on any Greek island and the second best in the whole country. He is a disciple of the revolutionary 'technomotion' style developed by Spain's star chef Andoni Luis Aduriz. He does not sell food but emotions; he doesn't nourish the stomach but the soul. The menu changes often and has offered such delicacies as medallions of fish in triple-sec with sesame, lamb simmered with cumquats and olive-oil or tomato ice-cream. In spite of his fame,

set meals are available from as low as 60 euros. *May–Oct; daily, in the evening | On the road from Dassiá to Áno Korakianá | tel. 26 61 09 33 62 | Expensive*

KARIDIÁ

A high-class taverna with excellent service and many Greek dishes freshly prepared every day; tasty lamb specialities, excellent salads and pleasant house wines. *Koloktihópita*, puff pastry filled with courgette, is one of the house's vegetarian specialities. *Daily, in the evening | Dassiá | On the main road | Moderate*

MALIBU BEACH CLUB

Modern bar with a sunbathing lawn on the beach and music for the young. Snacks. *Daily | Between the hotels Dassia Beach and Dassia Chandris | Budget*

PANORAMA ☼

The name of this restaurant, with its large terrace high up on one of the hills in Dafníla, is well chosen: from here, you have a wonderful view over the island.

MARCO POLO HIGHLIGHTS

The many Corfiot specialities are also delightful. *Daily | Follow the signpost on the main road to the Hotel Daphníla Bay and then the restaurant signs | Expensive*

SPORT & BEACHES

The only beach worth mentioning on the Komméno Peninsula occupied by Dafníla is near the Hotel Corfu Imperial. The main, mostly pebbly beach at Dassiá is around 700 m long. There is no beach road to disturb your bathing in the midst of verdant nature. *Ágios Nikólaos Beach* between Dassiá and Dafníla has a 300 m stretch of sand. It is also the site of the – easily recognisable – country estate of the Russian oligarch Roman Abramovich, one of the world's richest men. There are often even two large motor yachts anchored in front of his high-security residence.

There are three good water-sport centres on the main beach in Dassiá with two others on the hotel beaches at Daphníla Bay and Corfu Imperial.

ENTERTAINMENT

EDEM

This beach bar is also open during the day and there are several large beach parties with fireworks in July and August. *Daily | Dassiá | In front of the Hotel Schería, approx. 100 m north of the terminus for bus number 7*

TARTAYA

Exotic atmosphere in this lounge bar with its palm trees lit in orange. Every corner of the mainly open terrace is different and numerous mirrors create unexpected effects. You can make yourself comfortable on the stools and chairs, in a hammock, or just strike up new friendships at the bar. *Daily | Dassiá | On the main road north of the Chandris Hotel*

WHERE TO STAY

DASSIÁ BEACH

What makes this three-storey hotel, hidden between the trees, so special is its location only 10 m from the sea. Shortly after it was built, a law was passed forbidding hotels to be constructed less than 50 m from the water. That is why it is difficult to find a hotel in such a privileged location.

The owner's family is omnipresent and supervises the charmingly old-fashioned service. The rooms are simply but tastefully furnished. Under its densely leafed roof, the hotel taverna lies between the only 2 m-wide beach promenade and the hotel entrance. It is also open to the public and serves a wide range of typical food and grilled dishes at reasonable

Pure luxury: the Grecotel Corfu Imperial occupies almost all of the Komméno Peninsula

prices. The hotel has a bathing jetty and the next water-sport centre is only 50 m away; the main street with its cafés and bars, approximately 300 m. *54 rooms | Dassiá | On the main beach | tel. 26 61 09 32 24 | www.dassiahotels.gr | Moderate*

DASSIÁ CHANDRIS
The main attraction of this architecturally unspectacular hotel is its expansive garden on the main beach in Dassiá. *251 rooms and bungalows | tel. 26 61 09 33 51 | www. chandris.gr | Expensive*

GRECOTEL CORFU IMPERIAL ★
Pure luxury: the Grecotel Corfu Imperial occupies most of the Komméno Peninsula. Nowhere is more luxurious than this for your stay on Corfu. The house owned by the German-Greek *Grecotel* hotel chain takes up an entire peninsula, has its own water-sport centre, private bays with three sandy beaches, a large freshwater pool, as well as an indoor swimming pool. The presidential villas have their own pools and yacht moorings. *308 rooms | Dafníla (signposted) | tel. 26 61 09 14 81 | www.grecotel.gr | Expensive*

NEFÉLI ☆
Peaceful, informal hotel with pool in a large garden. Some of the rooms are decorated according to various Corfiot themes. The restaurant offers enchanting panoramic views. The closest sandy beach is 800 m away on foot. Renting a car is recommended. *Komméno Peninsula | tel. 26 61 09 10 33 | www.hotelnefeli.com | Moderate*

WHERE TO GO

ÁNO KORAKIÁNA (126 C3) (*ℳ C 3–4*)

With its 900 inhabitants and 37 (usually closed) churches and chapels, Áno Korakiána is one of Corfu's largest mountain villages. Just a brief stroll along the main road will reveal any number of historical buildings: round portals and houses built over the street, beautiful doorframes and windowsills with stone carvings, most of them from the Venetian period. House number 288 on the main street (Odós Dimokratías) is particularly striking with its rich ornamentation of bizarre sculptures. It used to be the house of a local sculptor; unfortunately, nothing else is known about him. Visit Áno Korakiána late in the afternoon when the old-fashioned cafés are open and the streets are full of life. *6 km (3.7 mi) from Dassiá*

ÍPSOS & PIRGI (127 D3–4) (*ℳ C–D 4*)

These two coastal resorts merge into one another, lack character and are at best, average. Holidaymakers sun themselves on the – at most – 5 m-wide strip of shingles directly below the busy main island road; the other side of the road is lined with mediocre bars, restaurants, souvenir shops and roads to the camping sites. However, there is one culinary bright spot: the INSIDER TIP *Grand Balcon Restaurant (daily | North of Ípsos above the road to Barbáti | Moderate)* that serves mostly specialities from the north of mainland Greece. Here, *chtapódi*, octopus, is still prepared as the typical Corfiot *bourdéto*. Another highlight for connoisseurs is *katsikáki gástras*, kid (of the goat variety!) cooked in a clay pot. In winter, wild boar is served. *2 km (1.2 mi) from Dassiá*

INSIDER TIP SOKRÁKI ✷ (126 C3) (*ℳ C3*)

Driving to Sokráki is quite an experience if you take the road from Áno Korakiána. The tarmac road is mostly only single-lane and winds itself like a corkscrew up a steep slope with 23 hairpin bends and even more gentle ones revealing breathtaking views of central and southern Corfu. The passengers usually have sweaty hands when they finally reach Sokráki and the driver will need to shake out his arms after all the hard work.

The best place to do that is on the tiny village square where two, quite unspoilt cafés serve salads with *fétta* (cheese made of sheep's or goat's milk). 😊 INSIDER TIP Both of them also offer *tzizimbírra*, the special Corfiot ginger beer, from the middle of May. If you order this, you will enjoy something that is unique in the whole of Greece. *11 km (6.8 mi) from Dassiá*

GUVIÁ & KONTOKÁLI

(127 D4–5) *(⫟ C–D 4)* **You will feel like you are on a mountain lake in Switzerland on the shore in Guviá (pop. 950) and Kontokáli (pop. 1600).**

The bay of Guviá is almost completely surrounded by green hills; olive groves reach down to the water. Looking through the bay entrance, you will be able to make out the mountains in the province of Épiros on the mainland that are covered

seem out of place and rather neglected; however, these buildings, which are now in ruins, were full of life in the last 20 years of Venetian dominance over Corfu. This is where ships were built, repaired and put into dry dock over winter. *Free access | Between the main beach and marina, well signposted in the village*

FOOD & DRINK

KAPETÁNIOS/CAPTAIN
Small, traditional, informal restaurant away from the hustle and bustle; good, home-style Greek food and fresh fish.

It has been a long time since ships were built here: the Venetian shipyards in Guviá

with snow until well into April. In Corfu's largest yacht harbour in the bay between Guviá and Kontokáli, you can breathe in the atmosphere of the big wide world.

SIGHTSEEING

VENETIAN SHIPYARDS
Today, the walls, arches and entrance portal of the shipyard constructed in 1778

Daily, in the evening | In the village centre between the beach and village road; above the Hotel Sirena (look for the advertising board on the hotel roof) | Budget

MEDÚSA
Typical Greek *ouzeri* offering many specialities including Cypriot *scheftaliá*, minced-meat sausage in the stomach lining of a lamb, Corfiot country-style sausages and

pickled octopus. Children can have half portions at half the price. *Daily, in the evening | On the village road to Kontokáli | Moderate*

ROÚLA 🍴

This taverna lies far from the madding crowd on a side arm of the bay with a view of the yacht harbour and mountains. Mikhail Gorbatschov, Nana Mouskouri, Vicky Leandros and many Greek VIPs have enjoyed fish and lobsters here in an informal, simple setting. *Daily, in the evening; Sat & Sun, open for lunch | On the same peninsula as the Hotel Kontokáli Bay that is signposted on the main road | Expensive*

INSIDER TIP ▶ TÁKIS

This simple taverna on the village street in Kontokáli with tables in front of and behind the house has been in existence for a long time. The innkeeper is especially proud of his smoked trout from the Greek mainland. Lamb and *kokorétsi* are often grilled on a spit in the evening. Good English breakfast. *Daily; usually closed in the afternoon in July and August | Moderate*

SHOPPING

VASSILÁKIS ☺

Here you can taste and buy the products made by the distillery and winery of the same name. *Daily 8am–10pm | Guviá, on the road towards Dassiá*

BEACHES

The most beautiful beach in Kontokáli is located directly in front of the Hotel Kontokáli Bay and, like all other beaches in Greece, is open to the public. All of the other beaches between Kontokáli and Guviá were sacrificed for the construction of the marina. Guviá now only has a 200 m-long main beach and a strip

beneath the Louis Corcyra Hotel; both are mostly pebbly.

ENTERTAINMENT

ADONIS CLUB

Small cellar disco. *Daily | Village road towards Kontokáli*

WHERE TO STAY

ILIÁDA BEACH

A hotel in the centre of town near the main beach with pool and a relaxed atmosphere. Its proximity to the marina makes it particularly attractive for crews from the yachts. *54 rooms | Guviá | tel. 26 61 09 13 60 | www.gto.gr | Moderate*

KONTOKÁLI BAY

This hotel welcomes families and is located on a small peninsula between Kontokáli and the island capital 6 km (3.7 mi) away. Apart from some occasional aircraft noise it is quietly located. There are free sun beds and umbrellas for the guests on two sandy beaches and around the seawater pool. Mountainbikes, two tennis courts and various water sports are available at a charge. *259 rooms | Kontokáli | tel. 26 6109 05 00 | www.kontokalibay.com | Expensive*

LOUIS CORCYRA BEACH

Beach hotel that welcomes children in a spacious garden with tennis, squash and a fine range of water sports. *265 rooms | tel. 26 61 09 01 96 | www.louishotels.com | Expensive*

WHERE TO GO

ÁGIOS IOÁNNIS (127 D5) (𝘔 D5)

Aqualand, Corfu's first fun pool, is located in this inland village on the connecting road between Kérkyra and Paleokastrítsa (see p. 107).

The small INSIDER TIP Pension *Marida* on the square in the historical centre is a peaceful refuge where you can stay in a country house, built in 1823 and set in a large garden, well away from any touristy hustle and bustle *(13 rooms | tel. 26 61 05 24 10 | Budget). 5 km (3.1 mi) from Guviá* completely undeveloped, the village absolutely untouched. That is all over now, but Pélekas has still kept something of its charm. Most of the tourists up in the mountain village are backpackers; the restaurants and cafés are simple and small. There is still the typical grocery store with

The church and taverna are at the heart of every Corfiot village: evening in Pélekas

PÉLEKAS, GLIFÁDA & MIRTIÓTISSA

(126–127 C–D6) (∅ C5) **The small mountain village Pélekas (population 565) used to be an insider's tip for hippies.** The three beaches in the parish were

the gossipy owner and excursion buses do not stop in the village.

The several-metre-high cement wall that runs for kilometres along the access roads is sprayed with ● colourful graffiti – often of artistic value; the other walls in the village have also been imaginatively decorated during the several graffiti festivals. Two of the three beaches are firmly in the grip of mass tourism. There are several large hotels at *Glifáda Beach* and the first was opened at *Pélekas Beach* in 1999. At *Mirtiótissa Beach* there is only one single taverna and a monastery. The parish promotes a stay in the mountain village: during the high season in the summer, a small bus travels, free of charge, between Pélekas and the beach at Glifáda – that is, if the council has approved the budget for that year.

There is an excellent website for the foreign community in Pélekas that is not restricted to the village itself. *www.pelekas.com*

SIGHTSEEING

KAISER'S THRONE ★ ☼

During his stays on Corfu, Kaiser Wilhelm II was fond of a small rock on the top of the hill *(Sunset Point)* that towers above Pélekas where he sat and watched the sun set. Today, a signposted tarmac road leads up there from the village. In June it looks like a red ball of fire is rolling down the Corfiot hills when the sun seems to settle on a mountain top before continuing on its heavenly journey at the same angle as the slope.

PANAGÍA MIRTIÓTISSA (MONÍ MYRTTIDIÓN) MONASTERY

One of the most beautifully located monasteries on the island lies hidden between olive trees, banana plants and countless flowers – and it is only 200 metres from a nudist beach. According to legend, a Turk who had converted to Christianity founded it in the 14th century after he had discovered an icon of Maria in a myrtle bush. However, the present buildings date from the 19th century. Today, just one monk lives in the monastery; he keeps it in order and would like to revitalise the old oil mill. *Daily 9am–1pm and 5–9pm | Access via a narrow road, which is tarmaced at first and then cemented, that is off the road between Pélekas and the Rópa Valley; it is easy to miss the signpost! | Car park (chargeable) half way up; limited parking on the beach and near the monastery*

FOOD & DRINK

ALÉXANDROS ☼

The first taverna in the village opened in 1960 and is still one of the best. The service is friendly and it offers good value for money. *Daily | Pélekas, in the centre on the road to Kaiser's Throne | Moderate*

ELIÁ ☼

Snacks and standard dishes are served in the modern taverna about 10 minutes' walk from the beach; this is not the place for haute cuisine. A blackboard showing the monastery's opening times is hung opposite the taverna. *Daily | On the road to Mirtiótissa beach | Budget*

LEVANT ☼

The restaurant in the hotel of the same name on the hilltop above Pélekas serves Corfiot specialities such as the juicy ham *nouboúlo*, with *penne tricolore* or pumpkin in elegant surroundings. The baked noodles, *pastitsjo*, without the frequently stodgy Béchamel sauce, can also be recommended. You can sit on the large terrace of the restaurant even if you just have a drink. But maybe you should try the sweet Greek speciality *gliká koutalioú* (sweet spoon) – various fruit in syrup. *Terrace all day; restaurant daily, in the evening | Reservation recommended: tel. 26 61 09 42 30 | Expensive*

PÉTRA

The trendy café bar just above Pélekas Beach attracts Corfiots from all over the island. Cocktails and champagne are the drinks of the day and the snacks served are international. *Daily | Southern road to the beach | Expensive*

Crystal-clear water and a beautiful beach make Mirtiótissa Bay a bather's dream

SPORT & BEACHES

The secluded, approximately 300 m-long, ★ sandy beach at Mirtiótissa is unofficially used as a nudist beach. So far, only a limited number of sun beds and umbrellas have been available for hire but there is a certain amount of shade among the rocks. This beach is really something and well worth visiting, no matter where you are staying on Corfu.

Glifáda Beach, on the other hand, is usually very crowded but there are plenty of sun beds, umbrellas and water sport activities. Two narrow tarmac roads lead down to Pélekas Beach which is not quite as busy and is also suitable for children. There is a water-sport centre here too.

ENTERTAINMENT

The nightlife is concentrated in the cafes and bars around the village square.

PÉLEKAS CAFÉ ⚡

This modern café on the small main square is a meeting place for the locals and holidaymakers in the evening. The village priest even drops by regularly. There is Greek and international music and you have a good view of the island through the wide-open windows. The visitors' book is always open too and is full of praise for the friendly atmosphere. Daily | Pélekas

WHERE TO STAY

LEVANT ★ ⚡

The hotel's hillside location is unique on Corfu. It has an inviting swimming pool and all rooms have panoramic views. There is also a computer room with internet access and a video collection. Unfortunately, the cleanliness of the rooms is not always up to scratch. Demand improvements! 25 rooms | Pélekas Sunset Point | tel.

26 61 09 42 30 | www.levant-hotel.com |
Expensive

PÉLEKAS COUNTRY CLUB

Suites and studios decorated with antiques on an 18th-century country estate with 125 acres of olive groves and gardens. Pool, helipad and excellent breakfast. *11 rooms | 8 km (5 mi) on the road from Kérkyra to Pélekas | tel. 22 61 05 22 39 | www.country-club.gr | Expensive*

INSIDER TIP ▶ TÉLLIS AND BRIGITTE

Crystal-clear water and a beautiful beach make Mirtiótissa Bay a bather's dream. The German-Greek hosts and their sons, Spíros and Níkos, take exceptional care of their guests. They will gladly join you for a glass of wine or ouzo and sometimes let you help at the barbecue. ☼ The rooms at the back of the house offer a beautiful view over the island. Hikers on the Corfu Trail are given special discounts! *8 rooms | In the centre of Pélekas, signposted on the main road | tel. 26 61 09 43 26 | www.pelekas.com | Budget*

THOMAS BY G & G

Two Italian brothers run this well-established guesthouse in a relaxed manner. All the rooms have balconies and the owners have set up an Italian-Greek restaurant on the ground floor that is open in the high season. *16 rooms | On the road to Kaiser's Throne | tel. 69 79 20 84 30 | www.thomas pelekas.com | Budget*

WHERE TO GO

ÉRMONES
(126 C5) (*ଢ C5*)

Today, as in ancient times, Homer's Odysseus would certainly rub his eyes in disbelief, awakening out of a deep sleep on the beach at Érmones after his 10-year journey home. Maybe he would see a bathing beauty as lovely as Nausicaa, the daughter of King Alcinous of Phaeacia, standing in front of him. However, he would certainly not recognise the surroundings. The hinterland is now covered with a sprawl of hotels and guesthouses. Odysseus would be equally surprised to see the funicular that ferries guests staying at the *Grand Mediterraneo Resort Hotel* from their rooms high up on the slope down to the beach, which — at just 200 m long — is not really one of Corfu's most beautiful. More attractively priced accommodation can be found at *Hotel Elena (28 rooms | tel. 266 109 4131 | Moderate). 7 km (4.3 mi) from Pélekas*

LITTLE ORANGES

Corfu's most famous speciality is the ● cumquat. Corfu is the only place in Europe where they are grown as a cash crop. The fruit – which is the size of a small plum and originally came from China – was first brought to the island by the British in the first half of the 19th century. Like oranges, they mature in winter and can be picked between January and March. Corfiot companies use them to make various liqueurs: a colourless one from the flesh of the fruit and one that is bright pink from the skins. Cumquats are often made into jam, sold candied and can be eaten fresh during the harvest. The skin can be eaten as well; it gives the fruit its tangy aroma.

RÓPA VALLEY
(126 C4–5) (𝄜 C 4–5)

The terrace of the Corfu Golf Club restaurant is open to all and you will feel as if you are in an English park. The small modern chapel next to it is the only hint that you are actually in Greece. *6 km (3.7 mi) from Pélekas*

SINARÁDES
(128 A–B 1–2) (𝄜 C–D 6)

Outside Kérkyra, museums are few and far between. The ★ *Folklore Museum* in Sinarádes (pop. 1120) is a ray of light in this cultural desert. The exhibition on the two floors of this historical building, which was occupied as a house until 1970, shows how the Corfiots lived and worked in the country between 1860 and 1960. There are excellent descriptions of all the exhibits in English. Among the unique objects to be seen are two birth chairs and figures for the Greek shadow play *karagıóssi (Mon–Sat 9am–2pm | Entrance 2 euros | Signposted at the church; leave your vehicle at the car park in the village centre).*

It is worth taking a short stroll through the village with its many old houses after you have visited the museum. Those that are almost completely overgrown with flowers are particularly lovely. If you want to soak up the down-to-earth, local atmosphere, have a drink in one of the old-fashioned grocery stores-cum-*kafenía* on the road and watch village life go by. You will get plenty of this, too, in the simple **INSIDER TIP** Snackbar *Locanda (Budget)* on the *platía*, the village square. Stelíos, the proprietor, used to be a sailor and now organises the barbeque for his guests in the evening. In the high season, his wife prepares the specialities *pastitsáda* and *sofríto* every day.

If you like rabbit, you should visit the **INSIDER TIP** Taverna *Aerostáto* (call first).

Dímitri, the father, breeds the animals himself and slaughters them as needed. His son, Stávros, a model-plane builder and his wife Chríssa serve wine from the barrel *(daily from 10am | tel. 26 61 05 41 62 | Outside the village, high above the sea | Signposted on the road between*

Hidden behind a modest façade: the Folklore Museum in Sinarádes

Pélekas and Sinarádes | Moderate). A walk along the small track that starts just above the taverna will take you down to a small, usually deserted, sandy beach in about 15 minutes. *6 km (3.7 mi) from Pélekas*

TRIPS & TOURS

The tours are marked in green in the road atlas, pull-out map and on the back cover

1 AN UNUSUAL WALKING TOUR AROUND KÉRKYRA

On this stroll you will remain within the boundary of the island's capital but will experience its rural side far away from traffic. It not only offers beautiful natural scenery but also historical treats and will take you to a monastery as well as a lush, green bay for swimming. Time: 3–4 hours.

This walk with INSIDER TIP temple ruins and a sea view begins at the Corfu Stadium next to the airport. You can reach it on the number 2 bus. Starting out from the eastern side of the stadium, the route takes you first of all to the main cemetery with its church → p. 37 which you cross. A very narrow lane with some plain farm-houses leads out of the cemetery on the other side. Sheep graze, chickens peck and dogs laze about in the sunshine. After 100 m, you will reach the only remains of Corfu's ancient city wall from the 5th century BC on the left.

A few minutes later, you will come across the scanty remains of the ancient **Artemis Temple** → p. 36; Germany's Emperor Wilhelm II was especially interested in its excavation. It is right in front of the walls of the **Ágii Theodóri convent** → p. 40. One of the nuns who lives there will be pleased to show you the convent church. Stay on the small lane and turn right onto

Experience something new every day: interesting tours on Corfu as well as two boat trips to Páxos and the neighbouring country of Albania

the main road, go past the agricultural research institute for olive cultivation and a classicistic primary school and you will find yourself in front of the entrance to Mon Repos → p. 39 Castle Park. Here, you can admire the view of the romantic, old walls from the wonderful, green area surrounding the Paléopolis Basilica → p. 40 before you go in. Start off by visiting the small castle and then follow the signs to the Doric Temple. At the first junction,

take the shady path through the woods down to a small bay, completely enclosed by trees, with a wooden bathing jetty where you can take a quick dip.

The main path will take you past what is left of the Hera Temple to the extremely romantic foundations of an unnamed Doric temple from the 5th century BC. Some of its columns have been re-erected amidst the greenery and make a good photo opportunity. A path starting at the southeast corner of the temple area takes you to the low wall surrounding the castle park. If you climb over it and keep to the right on the path along the wall you will reach the tiny hamlet of Análipsi.

Here, you can follow the tarmac path along the castle wall back to the entrance of town and either take the bus back to the centre of town, climb up to Kanóni → p. 38, or walk through the suburb of Anemómilos with the Byzantine church Ágios Jáson ke Soccípatros → p. 34 to the coastal road.

Church without a congregation: the ghost village of Paleó Períthia

2

ONCE AROUND PANTOKRÁTOR

A good tarmac road leads up to Corfu's highest mountain. The peaceful villages around the mountain invite you to take a rest and there is also enough time for a swim. The tour from and back to Kérkyra is 110 km (68 mi) long and will take at least 12 hours.

Your day in the mountains begins at the large village of Áno Korakiána → p. 86. From here, follow the signs to Sokráki and Zigós. The road now becomes narrower and winds like a corkscrew up the steep slope. When you arrive in Sokráki → p. 86, you might need to stop for a coffee or a glass of the typical Corfiot lemonade called *tzizimbírra*. Then drive up a bit further and start ascending the flank of Pantokrátor. Let yourself be tempted to take a break in the taverna under a more than 200-year-old elm tree in Strinílas → p. 59. The entire island of Corfu lies spread out beneath you when you reach the summit of Pantokrátor → p. 58.

The next destination is Ágios Spirídonas → p. 52 where you can choose to go for a swim and have something to eat. But, you might prefer to have lunch in the next village: the old Venetian settlement of Paleó Períthia → p. 53 in a high valley at the foot of Pantokrátor. After a stroll through the ghost village, carry on to Kassiópi → p. 59 on the coast. The best way to soak in the beauty of this place is to walk around the promontory; this will take about 25 minutes.

Drive back to the south along the coast road. Kulúra → p. 63 and Kalámi → p. 62 are at least worth a quick look and a photo. However, you should definitely drive down to the old harbour in Nissáki → p. 58 and let the day come to a close on the INSIDER TIP terrace of a taverna near the sea or go to the tiny beach for a last dip.

Impressive bird's-eye view – but you can also walk around Kassiópi

3 SHOPPING BETWEEN GUVIÁ AND PALEOKASTRÍTSA

The shops along the main road on the east coast from Guviá to Paleokastrítsa will tempt you to buy some souvenirs or look over the shoulders of the craftsmen at work. Distance: 12 km (7.5 mi).

Soon after turning off the road around the island at Guviá → p. 87, you can stock up with delicious baked Corfiot goods at the Emeral Bakery on the left. A good kilometre further on, you will arrive at Sofoklís Ikonomídis and Sissy Moskídu's Ceramic Workshop where they create and fire colourful ceramic objects on the premises. After another 2.6 km (1.6 mi),

visit the olive-wood carving exhibition on the left of the road followed, after only 900 m on the right, by the Mavromátis Distillery, where the company's liqueurs can be purchased in the modern, air-conditioned showroom.

600 m further on, a no-through-road off to the left to Hotel Fundána will lead you past a traditionally painted country house. This is where Níkos Sakális produces and sells high quality INSIDER TIP leather bags, glasses cases, backpacks and book covers (follow signs to 'Leather Workshop'). All of his products bear the 'Seminole' trademark. The visit to the leather workshop ends our shopping tour. Perhaps now you're ready for a relaxing swim, or just enjoy the countryside or a bit of culture with a visit to Paleokastrítsa → p. 63 Monastery.

4 **BOAT TRIP TO PÁXOS ISLAND** ●

Páxos is only one twelfth the size of Corfu but, just like its big sister, it is also covered with olive groves. This boat trip will not only show you the island town of Gáios but also the impressive towering coastline and sea caves. There is often a stopover at the much smaller island of Antípaxos, which is only inhabited in summer, for a swim. Departures: daily from Kérkyra, Messongí-Moraítika and Kávos; Price. approx. 35 euros. Time: 8–9 hours.

The **Ipapánti Grotto** is the first highlight on this trip around the island; small boats can even go into it. In World War II, a Greek submarine lay in hiding there for months. The arrow-like pinnacle of the **Orthólithos** rock rising out of the sea is a popular photo spot. You will have plenty of time to wander through the streets of the main town, **Gáios**, and have

a meal at one of the tavernas on the *platía* at the harbour. From your table, you will be able to see the neighbouring island, **Ágios Nikólaos**, and through a narrow inlet the ruins of a Venetian fortress. The small island of **Panagía,** with its snow-white church dedicated to the Virgin Mary – the site of an annual pilgrimage with thousands of followers – borders to the north. Some of the excursion boats sail from Gáios to the village of **Párga** on the mainland (instead of cruising around the island) where you can either go for a swim or walk up to the medieval castle.

5 **BOAT TRIP TO ALBANIA**

Corfu's northeast coast doesn't face Greece, but Albania. Until 1990, this neighbouring country was completely cut off from Corfu, but now ferries and hydro-

The boat takes you to Gáios on Corfu's little sister island

foils travel daily between the two. This excursion will take you to a country in which, so far, almost nobody spends their holidays and to the most magnificent archaeological sites in the region. Departures: daily at 9am from Kérkyra, price: 38 euros (return ticket), duration approx. 9 hours, passport required.

Depending on the ferry, the crossing takes from 30 to 75 minutes and ends in the small town of Sarande, which the Greeks call Agía Saránda, in Albania. Although it only has 35,000 inhabitants, the many new eight-to-ten-storey buildings give it the appearance of being much larger. However, there is no life in many of the apartments; Albanians working abroad have bought them as an investment and are seldom here. It is only a 10-minute walk from the ferry harbour along the narrow city beach and shore promenade to the new harbour that, with its cafés, is the most attractive area of Sarande. After leaving the harbour, walk past the Hotel Porto Edo on the left and then turn left at the first crossing. This will lead you to the town's main square with a small green area and the fenced-in ruins of the early-Christian Ágia Saránda Basilica from the 6th century. This is also the site of the tourist information office and taxi rank. If you haven't already booked a bus excursion, you can make a tour by taxi with a one-hour stop at your destination for 30–40 euros.

The 24 km (15 mi) road takes you past substantial building activity to the narrow strip of land between the sea and Lake Butrint. The entrance to the excavation site of ancient Butrint lies next to the Vivarit Channel that connects the lake with the sea. The mountains you can see across the water are on mainland Greece. Butrint was founded around 1200 BC and was inhabited for more than 2800 years until well into the 16th century. It experi-

Remains from Albania's magnificent past: Ancient Butrint

enced its golden age in the Roman period and most of its – often, well preserved – historical monuments, which Italian archaeologists excavated and restored before World War II, date from that era. Today, Butrint is listed as a Unesco World Heritage Site *(daily 9am–6pm | Entrance: approx. 6 euros)*.

The excavation site is on a peninsula jutting into Lake Butrint that rises up to a height of 30 metres. It is densely wooded and the 50-minute walk seems like a stroll through a park. There are boards with detailed information in English, ground plans and sketches of the reconstruction of everything that can be seen here: Roman baths and a Roman theatre, the baptistery of an early-Christian basilica from the 5th/6th century that has been preserved up as far as roof level, the partially very well preserved city walls and several city gates from various periods.

SPORTS & ACTIVITIES

Corfu is not a typical destination for sports lovers but there is still plenty to do. The many protected bays on the east coast and the long, open beaches on the west are ideal for all kinds of water sports and for all levels of ability.

Divers will find fewer restrictions than elsewhere in Greece and the numerous small roads and winding tracks are perfect for mountainbikers. And, along with Rhodes and Crete, Corfu is one of the three Greek islands with an 18-hole golf course.

BUNGEE BALL

Two brave people sit next to each other in a ball hanging from a cable at the Bungee Rocket in Kávos. With the same acceleration a car would need to reach 150 km/h in one second, the ball is shot to a height of 72 m (235 ft), rotates around itself a few times and then comes back to the starting position. *Daily, from 8pm | Approx. 50 euros per start | Kávos | On the main road*

CRUISES

You can take a short cruise lasting one or several days around Corfu on a variety of boats. *Corfu Yachting* in the marina at Guviá offers the greatest range of tours *(tel. 22 61 09 94 70 | www.corfuyachting. com)*.

Whether for the masses or the selected few, Corfu offers a great variety of sports – ranging from free-of-charge to fiendishly expensive

A one-day cruise on a wooden schooner from 1960 costs 90 euros per person (including lunch and drinks on board), and 75 euros on a sailing catamaran. Glass-bottomed boats and traditional *káikis* are also available. If you want real luxury, you can hire a sleek motor yacht – complete with captain – for six people for a hefty 3950 euros for 24 hours (drinks included here as well) and lap up the life of the jet-set for just one day.

After just a few brief explanations, you can set off on your rented motorboat with up to 30 HP without even having a licence. The hire company will tell you exactly where you are allowed to go. All boats are equipped with life jackets and a two-way radio. There are boat hire companies with the usual facilities in many resorts on the east and north coasts, as well as on the small neighbouring island of Páxos.

DIVING

There are very few restrictions on diving around Corfu making the area ideal for this sport. The best diving grounds are on the coast between Paleokastrítsa and Érmones. As this rocky area can only be reached from the land side at a few places, most of the dives start from boats. All diving centres on Corfu give individual instruction and organise dives for tourists. Most offer a full service for individual divers. *Korfu Diving Rolf Eyler | Paleokastrítsa | Ambeláki Bay | tel. 26 6304 16 04 | www.korfudiving.com* and *Calypso Diving | Ágios Górdis | At the southern end of the beach | tel. 26 61 05 31 01 | www.divingcorfu.com*

GOLF

Corfu has the greenest and most-cared-for 18-hole golf course in Greece. The high trees and small ponds give the course (par 72, length 6183 m) in the Ropa Valley its special atmosphere; the clubhouse with its restaurant and small pro-shop is another plus. Guests are welcome. Green fees: 90 euros per day; from 220 euros for 8 days. *Corfu Golf Club | tel. 26 61 09 42 20; in winter, tel.: 210 6 91 87 95 | www.corfu golfclub.com*

HIKING

With its many shady paths, green valleys and countless villages, Corfu is an ideal hiking region. You can never get completely lost because there is almost always a village in sight. The loveliest hikes run from south to north on the 222 km (138 mi) long, well-marked, INSIDER TIP *Corfu Trail* that goes from Cape Akotíri Arkoúdia to Cape Akotíri Ágias Ekaterínis. More information and links to hike organisers along this long-distance path: *www.corfutrail.org*

HORSE RIDING

The best-run riding stables on the island offer tours for beginners and experts: INSIDER TIP *Trailriders, near Áno Korakiána, signposted | Mon–Sat 10am until noon and 5 until 7pm | Free transfers in the region between Paleokastrítsa and Gouviá | tel. 26 63 02 30 90 | www.trailriderscorfu. com*

MIND, BODY & SPIRIT

The range of spa facilities on offer on Corfu is rather mediocre with only a few of the larger hotels having these. However, the island is first-rate if you are interested in far-eastern practices such as yoga and meditation and you will find many organisers based along the coast between Ágios Geórgios Pagón and Arillás.

MOUNTAINBIKING

Two companies offer INSIDER TIP guided mountainbike tours with various levels of difficulty. They, and some other smaller firms, also have bikes for hire. Guided day tours start at 35 euros (10 % internet discount). *S-A-F Travel / Hellas Bike | Skombú (on the Guviá-Paleokastrítsa road) | tel. 26 61 09 75 58; mobile 69 45 52 80 31; The Corfu Mountainbike Shop | Dassiá | 150 m north of Hotel Dassiá Chandris on the main road | Branch office in Grecotel Daphnília Bay | tel. 26 61 09 33 44 | www. mountainbikecorfu.gr*

TENNIS

Most of the large hotels have tennis courts; some are also available to people not staying in the hotel. The best complex that is open year-round and very popular with Corfiots belongs to the Greek national team player Spíros Micháleff:

Daphníla Tennis Club | Near Grecotel Daphníla Bay | tel. 26 61 09 05 70

WATERSPORTS & YACHTING

There are water-sport centres at all of the main hotels and popular beaches. The bays between Dassiá and Kontokáli are particularly suited to waterskiing: a round costs about 25 euros. Here, there are also many kinds of fun rides (banana-ride, 18 euros/ride). Paragliding is also available on many beaches but there are great price differences depending on the season and centre. A solo glider pays between 35 and 45 euros; tandems, from 45 to 70 euros. Windsurfers, dinghy and catamaran sailors are drawn to the west coast where the winds are stronger. There are good centres in Paleokastrítsa, Ágios Geórgios Pagón and Érmones. Kite-surfing is only possible in Ágios Geórgios Pagón.

An extensive water-sport package deal is available to those staying at *San Giorgio* Hotel, with its uniquely beautiful park landscape, with equipment provided exclusively by the organiser.

Those with a license for open-sea sailing can rent yachts by the week – some with a skipper. *Corfu Yachting | Marina Guviá | tel. 26 61 09 94 70 | www.corfuyachting. com | Sal Yachting | Kérkyra | Odós Sp. Mouríki 3 | tel. 26 61 03 04 09 | www.sal yachts.gr*

Sailing with a historical background: Corfu offers courses for beginners and experts

TRAVEL WITH KIDS

Corfu is a problem-free destination for families with children. The little ones are welcome everywhere. The Greeks don't fuss about their children very much but simply let them take part in most adult activities – and let them stay up until well past midnight.

You can choose from a wide range of baby food, nappies and fresh milk in the supermarkets. There are reductions for children up to the age of 12 on bus services, ships and excursion boats, as well as at various events, and most of the large hotels have paddling pools. If you stay in a hotel or apartment without a pool, you will be welcome to use any hotel pool as long as you buy drinks and snacks at the bar.

However, some things could be better on Corfu: highchairs and special meals for children are rare and even car hire services hardly ever have child seats. There is a playground in almost every village but the equipment is usually in a poor state of repair. Despite this, there is often a lot going on here in the early evening when the sun has lost its strength and the stars start to emerge. There are no restrictions or fences to stop children playing in the ruins of Corfiot castles – but the pits and walls are also unsecured and not without their dangers.

A word about your first-aid kit: doctors often prescribe antibiotics to cure simple colds; if you don't approve of this, you

Photo: Fun snorkelling at Gardénos Beach

**The kids will have a great time –
fun for the whole family in the water
and on dry land**

should make sure you have your own
selection of medicine with you.

The flat, wind-sheltered bays on the east
coast are much better for children who
cannot swim than the beaches on the
west where the water quickly becomes
deep and there is often a slight swell and
strong undercurrents. The best beaches
for children are in the wide bay at Lefkími
and in Dassiá where the water is comparatively safe.

INSIDER TIP ▶ MINI DRIVERS
(U F4) (*D 5*)

On almost every summer evening between 7 and 10pm there is masses going
on at the southern end of the Esplanade.
This is where a child's dream comes true in
the form of small electric cars that can be
driven by anyone capable of holding a
steering wheel and reaching the pedals –

which sometimes proves easier than taking the foot off the accelerator. There is room in the cars for two children. It's a good idea to keep an eye on the little ones as there is no fence around the driving area: runaways can drive almost anywhere just as long as the battery holds out. Around 4 euros for 15 minutes of childhood bliss.

MINI-TRAIN ON WHEELS
(U E4) (*M D 5*)

Miniature trains with a locomotive and three carriages with room for around 20 people in each are popular throughout Greece. They travel on rubber tyres and run on electric motors. The *trenáki* – Greek for little train – in Kérkyra makes 40-minute tours along the coast road to Paleópolis every hour between 11am and 2pm, and 5 and 11pm. The station is in front of Hotel Arcadíon on the Esplanade;

the price is the same for everybody over the age of four: 5 euros.

SEA LION SHOW AND FISH-WATCHING WITH THE CALYPSO STAR ●

During the week, the *Calypso Star* leaves the Old Harbour hourly between 10am and 6pm – on Sundays from 11am to 4pm. The 18 m-long glass-bottomed boat with room for around 50 passengers heads to the island of Vídos off the north coast where it stops so that its guests can watch a show with trained sea lions. Some people may object to this show from an animal protection point of view. If enough people complain, it might be possible to drop this part of the programme.

There are large, glass windows in the hull of the ship and you will be able to watch the fish while the ship slowly steams ahead. These have become scarce in Greek waters and a diver attracts them with

Biking or swimming – it's more enjoyable together

food. You will almost always see a whole school of them – they know the *Calypso Star* and its diver. The 40-minute trip costs 16 euros for adults and 9 euros for children aged 2 to 11.

STARING PILOTS IN THE EYE ●
(127 E6) (*∅ D5*)

The airport runway in Corfu is at sea level. And Kanóni, the cape of Análipsis Peninsula, rises up only about 300 m from its southern end as the crow flies. You can sit up there on a café terrace and have a fine view of the planes coming in to land or preparing to take off. If the planes land from the south, you will almost be able to look straight into the pilot's eye – you are both on the same level.

It is just as fascinating to watch the planes turn at the southern end of the runway and see how they gain speed and then take off. Something else both young and old will enjoy up here: the refreshing sundaes are really a treat!

TOURS WITH A HORSE AND CART
(U F4 und C1) (*∅ D 5*)

You will often hear the clatter of hooves in Kérkyra from one of the many one-horse carriages pulled by colourfully decorated horses in the Old Town. There is enough room in them for four adults (or two adults and four small children). But, you will have to dig deep into your pockets: 30 minutes cost about 35 euros (try to bargter!). The carriages line up waiting for customers in front of the Schulenberg Monument on the Esplanade and, in the morning, at the Old Harbour. The best time to take a ride is in the early evening.

CENTRAL CORFU

AQUALAND WATER PARK

The second of the two adventure water parks on Corfu, extending over an area of 75,000 m², is located near the village of Ágios Ioánnis in the verdant centre of the island. It has spacious lawns for sunbathing and its several freshwater pools, including some with wave machines, invite you to take a dip, while numerous giant slides make sure you hit the water with a splash. There are self-service restaurants and bars and, if you like loud music all day long, just find a place near one of the loudspeakers. The number 8 bus leaves Kérkyra at 11am and 12.30, 2.15, 3.15 and 5pm and returns around 20 minutes later (tickets must be bought in advance at the kiosk). *May–Sept daily 10am–6pm | Admission: adults 25 euros; children (4–12 years of age) 17 euros; weekly pass 75 euros | www.aqualand-corfu.com*

THE NORTH

HAVE A SPLASH IN HYDROPOLIS
(127 D1) (*∅ C2*)

With its eight large water slides and numerous other facilities, this water park and its attractions on the eastern edge of Acharávi, similar to Aqualand in central Corfu, is a real magnet and fun for all the family. *Hydropolis. May–Sept daily 10am–7pm | Admission: adults, 16 euros; children (5–12 years of age) 10 euros | www.gelina village.gr*

A DRIVE THROUGH A LEMON GROVE
(127 D1) (*∅ C2*)

Children can go for a drive in miniature electric cars next to the Lemon Garden in Acharávi. When they pass their test, they get a lemon instead of a licence. The perfectly laid-out track is well equipped with safety in mind and parents will be able to relax and enjoy their cocktails or coffee in the neighbouring lemon grove while their children have fun. *Daily from 6pm | 30 min approx. 4 euros*

FESTIVALS & EVENTS

The Corfiot holiday calendar boasts many events that reveal Venetian and Orthodox influences. Here, the carnival is widely celebrated with many colourful balls, costume parties and parades. Holy Week and Easter closely follow the Orthodox tradition. The dates of these moveable feast days are different from other Christian churches. Church consecration festivals, which are celebrated in every village, form a symbiosis between the two. The Orthodox saints are lauded with music with an Italian touch on their feast day.

In Kérkyra in particular, there are numerous concerts and other cultural events throughout the summer season where you will be able to experience ancient tragedies and Greek rock music in open-air theatres and medieval castles.

HOLIDAYS

1 January (New Year's Day), **6 January** (Epiphany), **27 February, 2012 | 18 March, 2013** (Shrove Monday), **25 March** (National Holiday), **13 April, 2012 | 3 May, 2013** (Good Friday), **15/16 April, 2012 | 5/6 May, 2013** (Easter), **1 May** (Labour Day),

21 May (Union of the Ionian Islands with Greece), **3/4 June, 2012 | 23/24, June 2013** (Whitsun), **15 August** (Assumption of Mary), **28 October** (National Holiday), **25/26 December** (Christmas/Boxing Day).

FESTIVALS & EVENTS

6 JANUARY

▶ *Blessing of the Waters and Baptism of Christ:* Processions to the sea are held in all larger towns where a priest throws a cross into the waves. The young man who brings it back will be blessed by good fortune throughout the coming year.

FEBRUARY/MARCH

Carnival processions in Kérkyra on the last three Sundays and Wednesday before Shrove Monday.

SHROVE MONDAY

▶ INSIDER TIP High-spirited atmosphere with music and dancing in Messongí.

GOOD FRIDAY

Processions in all villages and in the capital, starting in the afternoon.

Something is always happening on the island – from the elaborate carnival celebrations to the church festivals in autumn

EASTER

● Holy Saturday: Corfiots throw hundreds of clay jugs filled with water from balconies and windows onto the main streets in the Old Town. This turns into a public festival with music and dancing.

At 11pm, monumental ▶ *Resurrection service* in all churches followed by fireworks Easter Sunday: grilled lamb in every village; traditional ▶ *family festival*.

MAY

20 and 21 May: ▶ *Church Consecration Festival* in honour of Saints Constantine and Helena in Nímfes.

JUNE

Folklore dances in the theatre on several evenings at the end of the school year.

EARLY JUNE–MID AUGUST

About 30 concerts – from rock to classical, from choral music to piano recitals – in his-torical locations such as the Old Fortress, St. George's Church and the University's Ionian Academy during the ● ▶ *International Festival of Corfu*. Usually free.

MID JULY

16/17 July: Church Consecration Festival in Benítses with music, dancing and small gifts for visitors.

Three-day ▶ *Cultural Festival* with plays and concerts in Gardíki Fortress on the second-to-last weekend in July.

AUGUST

10 August: Live music, boat processions and folklore during the ▶ *Barcarolle Festival* in the suburb of Garítsa.

14/15 August: ▶ *Church Consecration Festival* with music and dancing in Kassiópi and Paleokastrítsa.

23/24 August: ▶ *Church Consecration Festival* with music and dancing in the villages of Ágii Déka and Pélekas.

LINKS, BLOGS, APPS & MORE

LINKS

▶ www.greencorfu.com Website on nature and 'green' affairs on the island. The accompanying greencorfu.worldpress.com gives lots of information about local products, alternative forms of tourism and environmental awareness as well as a lot of other tips and advice for the ecologically minded

▶ www.allcorfu.com Comprehensive commercial website on all places on Corfu

▶ www.corfubeaches.com Informative site with news and reports on Corfu's beaches, with useful hints and many photos

▶ www.agni.gr Website in English of a taverna and travel agency in north-eastern Corfu; also, general information and a unique selection of – sometimes unusual – holiday homes; for example, an old olive mill or an ancient house on the harbour pier in Lóngos on the neighbouring island of Páxos

▶ www.corfu.gr With a mass on information on the island's history, climate and environment issues as well as what to do and where to eat

BLOGS & FORUMS

▶ corfubloggers.blogspot.com English blog by four women – three British and one Dutch – who have lived on Corfu for years and provide the latest news update

▶ www.corfublogs.gr Many selected Greek and English blogs on Corfu at a glance

Regardless of whether you are still preparing your trip or already in Corfu: these addresses will provide you with more information, videos and networks to make your holiday even more enjoyable.

VIDEOS & STREAMS

▶ www.corfuvisit.net The official site of the Corfu Town Council also presents videos including a 22-minute film about the island

▶ www.greeka.com Many videos including a 10-minute, 16 mm one about the island that was filmed in 1972

▶ www.corfu-tube.com If you manage to separate the grain from the chaff, you will find interesting videos made by visitors for visitors

APPS

▶ Corfu HiGuide This app not only provides information on Corfu but also on Mathráki, Erikoúsa, Páxos and Antipáxos. A recording or video on each sight can be downloaded. And, one advantage: you don't even need an internet connection

▶ iSlands Island hopping and excursion planning become easier with this app. Available in Greek and English

▶ Corfuguide The integrated map in this android app helps you find sights, hotels, restaurants and petrol stations. A calendar shows current events, and ferry connections make island hopping easy

NETWORKS

▶ twitter.com/GayCorfu This twitter blog of the private gaycorfuinfo.com portal gives news and information on gay events in summer

▶ www.facebook.com/pages/CORFU-EVENTS/307870969559 New, small community mainly concentrating on events on Corfu

▶ www.facebook.com/pages/corfu-paragliding/79007569977 Tips of all sorts are posted on the Corfu Paragliding Community pinboard and the latest information exchanged among sports freaks. Members also have fun posting their latest aerial pictures

TRAVEL TIPS

ARRIVAL

✈ Many airlines fly to Corfu in summer and there are flights via Athens throughout the year. The flight from London takes around 3¼ hours. Corfu's airport is on the outskirts of the town. You can easily take a taxi to your hotel or the coach terminal in Kérkyra. There are huge differences in the prices of flights and sometimes scheduled flights via Athens are cheaper than charters. The following sites can be recommended for more information: *www.ageanair.com, www.aua. com, www.easyjet.com, www.olympicair. com, www.ryanair.com*

🚢 In the summer months, there are several daily connections with the Italian ports of Ancona, Bari, Brindisi and Venice. Depending on the ship, the crossing to Brindisi takes from 3½–8 hours; to Ancona, around 20; and 29–36 hours to Venice. Compare prices at *www.gtp. gr, www.greekferries.gr, www.minoan.gr, www.superfast.com* or contact a travel agent. Travelling by bus or train to an Italian harbour is only advisable in exceptional cases.

BUSES

There are regular urban public bus services. You must purchase tickets in advance from kiosks, ticket machines or in your hotel. If possible, you should buy your tickets for long-distance buses/coaches at the bus station – if not, when you get on board.

CAMPING

Camping anywhere else but in a camp site is forbidden on Corfu. There are 13 official camp sites on the island – those in Dassiá, Káto Korakiána and Róda have a pool – but are only open in the summer season.

CAR HIRE

Bicycles, mopeds, motor scooters, motorbikes, 4x4s and cars can be rented in all of the holiday resorts on Corfu. An Vauxhall Corsa costs from around 35 euros per day. If you want to hire a car or motorbike, you have to be at least 23 years of age. Be careful: even if you have full insurance coverage, damage to the tyres and the underside of the car is not covered. No matter how small the accident, you should call the police – otherwise, the insurance company will not pay. And, if you rent a moped, it is a good idea to wear jeans even if the weather is hot; they will provide increased protection if you have a slight accident and fall.

RESPONSIBLE TRAVEL

It doesn't take a lot to be environmentally friendly whilst travelling. Don't just think about your carbon footprint whilst flying to and from your holiday destination but also about how you can protect nature and culture abroad. As a tourist it is especially important to respect nature, look out for local products, cycle instead of driving, save water and much more. If you would like to find out more about eco-tourism please visit: *www.ecotourism.org*

From arrival to time zones

Holiday from start to finish: the most important addresses and information for your Corfu trip

There is a good network of filling stations on the island and all sell both petrol and diesel. Most garages are open daily from 8am to 8pm. Self-service is still uncommon and coin-operated petrol stations are rare. Fuel prices are considerably higher than in many other countries in Europe.

The speed limit in built-up areas is 50 km/h and 90 km/h on main roads. It is compulsory to wear seatbelts in the front seats. The blood alcohol limit is 0.5; 0.2 for motorbike riders. The fines for traffic offences are extremely high. The police usually demand 60 euros for illegal parking that must be paid to the authority stated on the ticket.

CLIMATE, WHEN TO GO

The high season on Corfu lasts from May to October. Many hotels and most of the restaurants outside of the island's capital are closed in the other months. In May, the sea can still be too cold for swimming but this is the month when the flowers are at

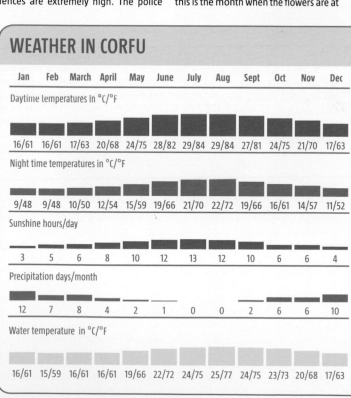

WEATHER IN CORFU

	Jan	Feb	March	April	May	June	July	Aug	Sept	Oct	Nov	Dec
Daytime temperatures in °C/°F	16/61	16/61	17/63	20/68	24/75	28/82	29/84	29/84	27/81	24/75	21/70	17/63
Night time temperatures in °C/°F	9/48	9/48	10/50	12/54	15/59	19/66	21/70	22/72	19/66	16/61	14/57	11/52
Sunshine hours/day	3	5	6	8	10	12	13	12	10	6	6	4
Precipitation days/month	12	7	8	4	2	1	0	0	2	6	6	10
Water temperature in °C/°F	16/61	15/59	16/61	16/61	19/66	22/72	24/75	25/77	24/75	23/73	20/68	17/63

their best. The water is pleasantly warm in autumn but by this time the vegetation is largely withered and burnt. It hardly rains between June and September but there are often very strong winds.

The capital, Kérkyra, is also an attractive winter destination. There are almost no holidaymakers during this period and the locals have time to enjoy themselves in the tavernas. There will be fires blazing in the open hearths in the bars, restaurants and cafés – and you will have the museums all to yourself!

CONSULATES AND EMBASSIES

BRITISH CONSULATE

18 Mantzarou Street 491 00, Kérkyra | tel.: 266 10-300 55 / 234 57 | fax: 266 10-379 95 | http://ukingreece.fco.gov.uk/en/

U.S. EMBASSY (ATHENS)

91 Vasilisis Sophias Avenue | 10160 Athens | tel.: (Main Switchboard/Info): 210 721 29 51 | http://athens.usembassy.gov | E-mail: athensamemb@state.gov

CUSTOMS

EU citizens can import and export goods for their personal use tax-free (800 cigarettes, 1 kg tobacco, 90 l of wine, 10 l of spirits over 22 %).

Visitors from other countries must observe the following limits, except for items for personal use. Duty free are: max. 50 g perfume, 200 cigarettes, 50 cigars, 250 g tobacco, 1 L of spirits (over 22 % vol.), 2 L of spirits (under 22 % vol.), 2 L of any wine. Gifts to the value of up to 175 euros may be brought into Greece.

There are special regulations for souvenirs from day trips to Albania: You may only bring back 40 cigarettes, 1 L of spirits or 2 L of wine.

DISCOTHEQUES

Greek discos do not usually open before 10 or 11pm. There is generally no entrance fee but the drinks are expensive; a long drink costs between 6 and 10 euros, a small bottle of beer 3 to 5 euros. There is no age check.

BOOKS & FILMS

▶ **My Family and Other Animals** – The famous animal film-maker and author Gerald Durrell's extremely humorous and much-loved description of his experiences on Corfu where he spent his childhood in the 1930s. The TV adaptation of this book was broadcast in 2005; it was directed by Sheree Folkson and is available on DVD

▶ **Fedora** – Billy Wilder's bizarre story of a Hollywood star who also spent some time on Corfu is much more sophisticated; with Hildegard Knef and Mario Adorf in the main roles.

▶ **For Your Eyes Only** – The James Bond adventure story begins off the coast of Corfu and parts of it were shot on the island in 1980.

▶ **Prospero's Cell: A Guide to the Landscape and Manners of the Island of Corfu** – His even more famous brother Lawrence Durrell captured the feeling of this period in his works of literature.

EMERGENCY SERVICES

112 for the police, fire brigade and ambulance; 171 for the tourist police

ELECTRICITY

Corfu has the same 220 volt as most continental European countries. You will need an adapter if you want to use a UK plug.

ENTRANCE FEES

National museums give discounts to pensioners over 65 years of age. Children from EU countries and students with an International Student Card are granted free admission. A joint ticket for the Archaeological Museum, Museum for Asian Art, the Byzantine Museum and Old Fortress is available at the ticket desk of any one of the four institutions for 8 euros. This represents a saving of 4 euros compared to the price of separate tickets.

There is no entrance fee for visiting churches and monasteries but donations are always welcome. The most discreet way to do this is to buy candles and light them in front of an icon with a prayer of intercession.

HEALTH

Well-trained doctors guarantee basic medical care. However, there is often a lack of medical equipment. The standard of the government hospital in Kérkyra is low. Complicated cases are sent to Athens. If you are seriously ill or injured, you should try to fly home.

Emergency treatment in hospitals and government health centres *(ESY, National Health Centre)* is free of charge. Theoretically, medical treatment from doctors in the state scheme is also free if you present the European Health Insurance Card issued by your own insurance company. However, in practice this is complicated and time-consuming. It is highly recommended that you take out an international health insurance; you can then choose your doctor, pay him in cash, get a receipt and then present your bills to the insurance company for refunding.

Chemists are well-stocked but do not always have British medication. In Greece, many branded medicines which are only available if you have a prescription in other countries, can be purchased without one and are cheaper than at home. These include painkillers and remedies for heartburn and herpes. You are only able to import small quantities to protect the financial interests of the pharmaceutical industry.

Mosquitoes also like Corfu. You should have mosquito protection in your first-aid kit as well as something for insect bites. Bathing shoes will protect you from sea urchins. There are no poisonous snakes or scorpions on the island.

IMMIGRATION INTO GREECE

A valid passport is required for entry into Greece. All children must travel with their own passport.

INFORMATION

GREEK NATIONAL TOURISM ORGANISATION

– *4 Conduit Street | London, W1S 2DJ | tel. 020 7495 9300*
– *www.visitgreece.gr; www.corfuvisit.net*

IONIAN ISLANDS TOURISM DIRECTORATE OFFICE

Open Mon to Fri 9am to 9pm; in July and August, also open on Saturdays. *Evagelistrias 4, 49100 Kerkyra | tel.: 26 61 03 75 20 | fax: 26 61 03 02 98*

INTERNET CAFÉS & WIFI

There are internet cafés in most holiday resorts. You can surf in comfort at Netoíkos near the Ágios Spirídonas Church in Kérkyra's Old Town *(daily 10am–midnight | Odós Kalogerétou 14 | tel. 26 61 04 74 91)*. In Greece a lot of hotels offer guests who have their own laptops free Wi-Fi access – at least in the lobby area. Some of the more expensive hotels however charge for this.

At the other end of the scale, an increasing number of cafés, bars and tavernas let their guests use this service free of charge; the transmission rate is usually very high.

LANGUAGE

The Greeks are proud of the characters in their language which are unique to Greece. Although place names and labels are often also written in Roman letters, it is still useful to have some knowledge of the Greek alphabet – and you really need to know how to stress the words correctly to be understood. The vowel with the accent is emphasised. The transcription of Greek names in the map section is based on the recommended international UN style. However, as this is seldom used in Greece itself, the text section of this guidebook is orientated on the standard pronunciation and spelling style used locally.

CURRENCY CONVERTER

£	€	€	£
1	1.10	1	0.90
3	3.30	3	2.70
5	5.50	5	4.50
13	14.30	13	11.70
40	44	40	36
75	82.50	75	67.50
120	132	120	108
250	275	250	225
500	550	500	450

$	€	€	$
1	0.70	1	1.40
3	2.10	3	4.20
5	3.50	5	7
13	9.10	13	18.20
40	28	40	56
75	52.50	75	105
120	84	120	168
250	175	250	350
500	350	500	700

For current exchange rates see www.xe.com

MONEY & CREDIT CARDS

The national currency is the euro. You can withdraw money from many cash machines with your credit or debit card. Banks and post offices cash traveller's cheques. Credit cards (especially Visa and MasterCard) are accepted by many hotels and restaurants but only by a few petrol stations, tavernas and shops. Bank opening hours are *Mon–Thur 8am–2pm, Fri 8am–1.30pm*

NEWSPAPERS

Foreign newspapers can usually be bought on Corfu one day after they appear. The English language weekly *Athens News* and monthly *The Corfiot* are published locally.

PHOTOS & FILMS

You can have digital photos burned on a CD in most photo shops or do it yourself in an internet café. Storage media and rechargeable batteries are available in photo shops but are expensive as are films and standard batteries. You need permission to take photos using a tripod or flash. Photographing is frowned upon in churches.

POST

There are post offices in Kérkyra and all major villages. It usually takes from 3 to 7 days for post to reach other European destinations. The large post offices always have a small selection of, often unusual, stamps.

Post offices are usually open from Mon to Fri from 7.30am to 8pm; in July and August they are normally also open for a few hours on Saturdays.

TAXI

There are plenty of taxis in Kérkyra. You can flag them down on the street, get in at the taxi ranks or telephone for one. The prices are set by the government and are comparatively low (e.g. Airport–town centre 8–12 euros). But, make sure that the taxi driver uses tariff 1 within the city limits; tariff 2 only applies to cross-country trips!

Outside the town, the taxis are officially called *agoraíon*. Their rates are the same as taxis but they do not have a meter. You pay a set price for a specific distance.

PHONE & MOBILE PHONE

Card phones are very common. You can buy telephone cards priced at 4 euros from the offices of the OTE telephone company and many kiosks.

With the exception of some emergency numbers, all Greek telephone numbers have ten digits. There are no area dialling codes. Greek mobile phone numbers always begin with '6'. Dialling codes: Greece 0030 followed by the telephone number.

BUDGETING

Taxi	1.17 euros *per kilometre*
Coffee	2.50 euros *a cup of coffee*
Pedal boat	10 euros *an hour*
Wine	3.50 euros *for a glass of wine*
Snack	2.20 euros *for gyros at a stand*
Petrol	1.60 euros *for 1 litre of super*

Code for Australia (0061), Canada (001), Ireland (00353), United Kingdom (0044), USA (001) followed by the area code without '0'.

Mobile phones are widely used. Reception is generally good except in some valleys. If you use a pre-paid Greek card you will not have to pay for incoming calls. These cards are available from the numerous shops run by the telecommunications companies such as Cosmote, Vodafone and Wind. The first time you buy a pre-paid Greek card, you will have to register by presenting your passport. Cards for reloading can also be purchased from many kiosks and supermarkets.

TIPPING

Like most other places in Europe, but at least 50 cents.

TIME

Greece is two hours ahead of Greenwich Mean Time, seven hours ahead of US Eastern Time and seven hours behind Australian Eastern Time.

USEFUL PHRASES GREEK

PRONUNCIATION

We have provided a simple pronunciation aid for the Greek words
(see middle column). Note the following:

'   the following syllable is emphasised

ð   in Greek (shown as "dh" in middle column) is like "th" in "there"

θ   in Greek (shown as "th" in middle column) is like "th" in "think"

Χ   in Greek (shown as "ch" in middle column) is like a rough "h" or
    "ch" in Scottish "loch"

A	α	a		H	η	i		N	ν	n
B	β	v		Θ	θ	th		Ξ	ξ	ks, x
Γ	γ	g, y		I	ι	i, y		O	ο	o
Δ	δ	th		K	κ	k		Π	π	p
E	ε	e		Λ	λ	l		P	ρ	r
Z	ζ	z		M	μ	m		Σ	σ, ς	s, ss

T	τ	t	
Y	υ	i, y	
Φ	φ	f	
X	χ	ch	
Ψ	ψ	ps	
Ω	ώ	o	

IN BRIEF

Yes/No/Maybe	ne/'ochi/'issos	Ναι/ Όχι/Ισως
Please/Thank you	paraka'lo/efcharis'to	Παρακαλώ/Ευχαριστώ
Sorry	sig'nomi	Συγνώμη
Excuse me	me sig'chorite	Με συγχωρείτε
May I ...?	epi'treppete ...?	Επιτρέπεται ...?
Pardon?	o'riste?	Ορίστε?
I would like to .../	'thelo .../	Θέλω .../
have you got ...?	'echete ...?	Έχετε ...?
How much is ...?	'posso 'kani ...?	Πόσο κάνει ...?
I (don't) like this	Af'to (dhen) mu a'ressi	Αυτό (δεν) μου αρέσει
good/bad	ka'llo/kak'ko	καλό/κακό
too much/much/little	'para pol'li/pol'li/'ligo	πάρα πολύ/πολύ/λίγο
everything/nothing	ólla/'tipottal	όλα/τίποτα
Help!/Attention!/	vo'ithia!/prosso'chi!/	Βοήθεια!/Προσοχή!/
Caution!	prosso'chi!	Προσοχή!
ambulance	astheno'forro	Ασθενοφόρο
police/	astino'mia/	Αστυνομία/
fire brigade	pirosvesti'ki	Πυροσβεστική
ban/	apa'gorefsi/	Απαγόρευση/
forbidden	apago'revete	απαγορέυεται
danger/dangerous	'kindinoss/epi'kindinoss	Κίνδυνος/επικίνδυνος

Milás elliniká?

"Do you speak Greek?" This guide will help you to say the basic words and phrases in Greek.

GREETINGS, FAREWELL

Good morning!/after-	kalli'mera/kalli'mera!/	Καλημέρα/Καλημέρα!/
noon!/evening!/night!	kalli'spera!/kalli'nichta!	Καλησπέρα!/Καληνύχτα!
Hello!/	'ya (su/sass)!/a'dio!/	Γεία (σου/σας)!/αντίο!/
goodbye!	ya (su/sass)!	Γεία (σου/σας)!
Bye!	me 'lene ...	Με λένε ...
My name is ...	poss sass 'lene?	Πως σας λένε;

DATE & TIME

Monday/Tuesday	dhef'tera/'triti	Δευτέρα/Τρίτη
Wednesday/Thursday	tet'tarti/'pempti	Τετάρτη/Πέμπτη
Friday/Saturday	paraske'vi/'savatto	Παρασκευή/Σάββατο
Sunday/weekday	kiria'ki/er'gassimi	Κυριακή/Εργάσιμη
today/tomorrow/yesterday	'simera/'avrio/chtess	Σήμερα/Αύριο/Χτες
What time is it?	ti 'ora 'ine?	Τι ώρα είναι;

TRAVEL

open/closed	annik'ta/klis'to	Ανοικτό/Κλειστό
entrance/	'issodhos/	Είσοδος/
driveway	'issodhos ochi'matonn	Είσοδος οχημάτων
exit/exit	'eksodhos/	Έξοδος/
	'Eksodos ochi'matonn	Έξοδος οχημάτων
departure/	anna'chorissi/	Αναχώρηση/
departure/arrival	anna'chorissi/'afiksi	Αναχώρηση/Άφιξη
toilets/restrooms / ladies/	tual'lettes/gine'konn/	Τουαλέτες/Γυναικών/
gentlemen	an'dronn	Ανδρών
(no) drinking water	'possimo ne'ro	Πόσιμο νερό
Where is ...?/Where are ...?	pu 'ine ...?/pu 'ine ...?	Πού είναι/Πού είναι ...;
bus/taxi	leofo'rio/tak'si	Λεωφορείο/Ταξι
street map/	'chartis tis 'pollis/	Χάρτης της πόλης/
map	'chartis	Χάρτης
harbour	li'mani	Λιμάνι
airport	a-ero'drommio	Αεροδρόμιο
schedule/ticket	drommo'logio/issi'tirio	Δρομολόγιο/Εισιτήριο
I would like to rent ...	'thelo na nik'yasso ...	Θέλω να νοικιάσω ...
a car/a bicycle/	'enna afto'kinito/'enna	ένα αυτοκίνητο/ένα
a boat	po'dhilato/'mia 'varka	ποδήλατο/μία βάρκα
petrol/gas station	venzi'nadiko	Βενζινάδικο
petrol/gas / diesel	ven'zini/'diesel	Βενζίνη/Ντίζελ

FOOD & DRINK

Could you please book a table for tonight for four?	Klis'te mass parakal'lo 'enna tra'pezi ya a'popse ya 'tessera 'atoma	Κλείστε μας παρακαλώ ένα τραπέζι γιά απόψε γιά τέσσερα άτομα
The menu, please	tonn ka'taloggo parakal'lo	Τον κατάλογο παρακαλώ
Could I please have ...?	tha 'ithella na 'echo ...?	Θα ήθελα να έχο ...?
with/without ice/ sparkling	me/cho'ris 'pago/ anthrakik'ko	με/χωρίς πάγο/ ανθρακικό
vegetarian/allergy	chorto'fagos/allerg'ia	Χορτοφάγος/Αλλεργία
May I have the bill, please?	'thel'lo na pli'rosso parakal'lo	Θέλω να πληρώσω παρακαλώ

SHOPPING

Where can I find...?	pu tha vro ...?	Που θα βρω ...?
pharmacy/ chemist	farma'kio/ ka'tastima	Φαρμακείο/Κατάστημα καλλυντικών
bakery/market	'furnos/ago'ra	Φούρνος/Αγορά
grocery	pandopo'lio	Παντοπωλείο
kiosk	pe'riptero	Περίπτερο
expensive/cheap/price	akri'vos/fti'nos/ti'mi	ακριβός/φτηνός/Τιμή
more/less	pio/li'gotere	πιό/λιγότερο

ACCOMMODATION

I have booked a room	'kratissa 'enna do'matio	Κράτησα ένα δωμάτιο
Do you have any ... left?	'echete a'komma ...	Έχετε ακόμα ...
single room	mon'noklino	Μονόκλινο
double room	'diklino	Δίκλινο
key	kli'dhi	Κλειδί
room card	ilektronni'ko kli'dhi	Ηλεκτρονικό κλειδί

HEALTH

doctor/dentist/ paediatrician	ya'tros/odhondoya'tros/ pe'dhiatros	Ιατρός/Οδοντογιατρός/ Παιδίατρος
hospital/ emergency clinic	nossoko'mio/ yatri'ko 'kentro	Νοσοκομείο/ Ιατρικό κέντρο
fever/pain	piret'tos/'ponnos	Πυρετός/Πόνος
diarrhoea/nausea	dhi'arria/ana'gula	Διάρροια/Αναγούλα
sunburn	ilia'ko 'engavma	Ηλιακό έγκαυμα
inflamed/ injured	molli'menno/ pligo'menno	μολυμένο /πληγωμένο
pain reliever/tablet	paf'siponna/'chapi	Παυσίπονο/Χάπι

POST, TELECOMMUNICATIONS & MEDIA

stamp/letter	gramma'tossimo/'gramma	Γραμματόσημο/Γράμμα
postcard	kartpos'tall	Καρτ-ποστάλ
I need a landline phone card	kri'azomme 'mia tile'karta ya dhi'mossio tilefoni'ko 'thalamo	Χρειάζομαι μία τηλεκάρτα για δημόσιο τηλεφωνικό θάλαμο
I'm looking for a prepaid card for my mobile	tha 'ithella 'mia 'karta ya to kinni'to mu	Θα ήθελα μία κάρτα για το κινητό μου
Where can I find internet access?	pu bor'ro na vro 'prosvassi sto índernett?	Που μπορώ να βρω πρόσβαση στο ίντερνετ?
socket/adapter/ charger	'briza/an'dapporras/ fortis'tis	πρίζα/αντάπτορας/ φορτιστής
computer/battery/ rechargeable battery	ippologis'tis/batta'ria/ eppanaforti'zomenni batta'ria	Υπολογιστής/μπαταρία/ επαναφορτιζόμενη μπαταρία
internet connection/ wifi	'sindhessi se as'sirmato 'dhitio/vaifai	Σύνδεση σε ασύρματο δίκτυο/WiFi

LEISURE, SPORTS & BEACH

beach	para'lia	Παραλία
sunshade/lounger	om'brella/ksap'plostra	Ομπρέλα/Ξαπλώστρα

NUMBERS

0	mi'dhen	μηδέν
1	'enna	ένα
2	'dhio	δύο
3	'tria	τρία
4	'tessera	τέσσερα
5	'pende	πέντε
6	'eksi	έξι
7	ef'ta	εφτά
8	och'to	οχτώ
9	e'nea	εννέα
10	'dhekka	δέκα
11	'endhekka	ένδεκα
12	'dodhekka	δώδεκα
20	'ikossi	είκοσι
50	pen'inda	πενήντα
100	eka'to	εκατό
200	dhia'kossia	διακόσια
1000	'chilia	χίλια
10000	'dhekka chil'iades	δέκα χιλιάδες

NOTES

FOR YOUR NEXT HOLIDAY ...

MARCO POLO TRAVEL GUIDES

ALGARVE
AMSTERDAM
BARCELONA
BERLIN
BUDAPEST
CORFU
DUBROVNIK &
  DALMATIAN COAST
DUBAI
EDINBURGH
FINLAND
FLORENCE
FLORIDA
FRENCH RIVIERA
  NICE, CANNES &
  MONACO

IRELAND
KOS
LAKE GARDA
LANZAROTE
LONDON
MADEIRA
  PORTO SANTO
MALLORCA
MALTA
  GOZO
NEW YORK

NORWAY
PARIS
RHODES
ROME
SAN FRANCISCO
STOCKHOLM
THAILAND
VENICE

- PACKED WITH INSIDER TIPS
- BEST WALKS AND TOURS
- FULL-COLOUR PULL-OUT MAP
  AND STREET ATLAS

ROAD ATLAS

The green line ▬ indicates the Trips & Tours (p. 94–99).
The blue line ▬ indicates the Perfect Route (p. 30–31).

All tours are also marked on the pull-out map

Photo: The harbour at Ágios Stéfanos

Exploring Corfu

The map on the back cover shows how the area has been sub-divided.
The page numbers refer to the different sections in the road atlas.

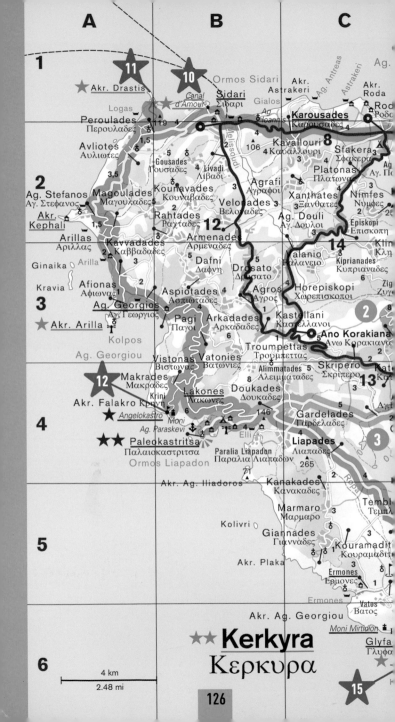

A

E F

4 km
2.48 mi

1

Akr. Kalamas

2

Akr. Vatatsas

Notio Steno Kerkyras
Notio Στενο Κερκυρας

Thyamis P.

Prasoudi

3

Igoumenitsa

Korakades
Κορακαδες

Kolpos Lefkimmis
Κόλπος Λευκίμμης

Akr. Lefkimmis

4

Petriti
Πετρίτη

Ag. Nikolaos
Αγ. Νικόλαος

Roumanades
Ρουμαναδες

Kaliviotis
Καλιβιότις

Molos
Μώλος

Ag. Joannis

Alikes
Αλυκες

Ag. Taxiarhes

Lefkimmi
Λευκιμμη

Athias
Αθιας

Perivoli
Περιβόλι

Ringlades
Ριγγλαδες

Potami
Ποταμι

Ano Lefkimmi
Ανω Λευκιμμη

Ag. Varvara

Ag. Aikaterini

Melikia
Μελικια

Lefkimm

5

Vitalades
Βιταλαδες

Ag. Anna

Kritika
Κρήτικα

Neohori
Νεοχωρι

Kavos
Καβός

Varvara
αρβαρα

Megahoros
Μεγαχωρος

Paleohori
Παλαιοχωρι

Akr. Kountouris

Gardenos

Ag. Markianos

Dragotina
Δραγωτινα

Spartera
Σπαρτερα

Ai Gardis Paleohoriou

Akr. Arkoudila

Moni
Panagias

Akr. Asprohavos

Paxos

6

129

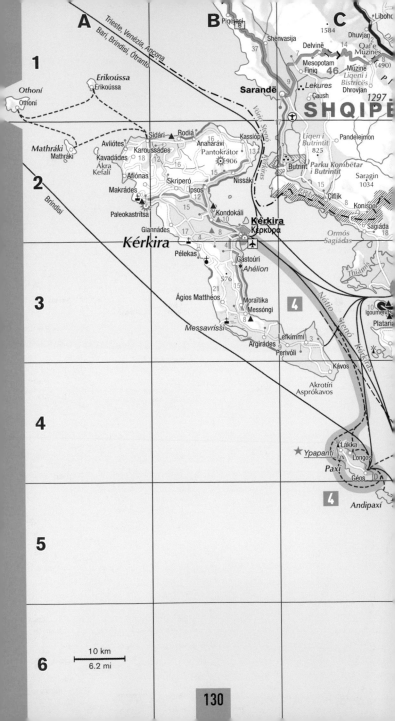

A Trieste, Venézia, Ancona
Bari, Brindisi, Otranto

B Pigerasi
Shënvasija
37
Delvinë
Dhuvjan
1584
14
Qaf'e
Müzines
(490)

C Liboho

1

Othoní
Othoní

Erikoússa
Erikoússa

Mesopotam
Finiq
Lekures
Çaush

Müzinë
Ligeni i
Bistricës
Dhrovjan

46

1297

Sarandë

SHQIPË

Mathráki
Mathráki

Sidári Rodiá
Avliótes
Karoussádes
Kavadádes 18 12
Ákra Afiónas
Kefalí
Makrádes
Skriperó
Ipsos
12

Anaharávi
Pantokrátor
906
16
15

Kassiópi
13

Liqen i
Butrintit
825

Pandelejmon

Nissáki

Butrint
Parku Kombëtar
i Butrintit

Saragin
1034

15
Çiflik
8
Konispol

2

Brindisi

Paleokastritsa

15
Kondokáli
10

Kérkira
Κέρκυρα

8
4

Giannádes
17 4

Kérkira

Pélekas

Gástoúri
Ahélion

576
21 15

Ormós
Sagiádas

Sagiáda
18

Thiámis

3

Ágios Matthéos

Moraïtika
Messóngi

4

Nótio Stenó Kerkíras

Igoumenits
Platariá

Messavríssi

8

Lefkímmi
3

Argirádes
Perivóli

Kávos

Akrotíri
Asprókavos

4

Ypapantí
Lákka
Longós

Paxí
Géos

4
Andipaxí

5

6

10 km
6.2 mi

130

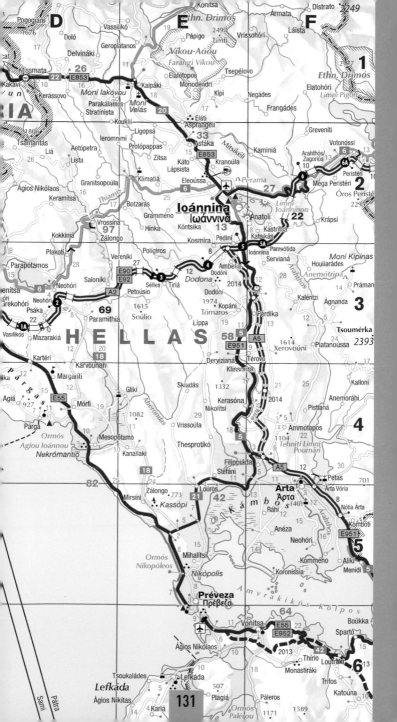

KEY TO ROAD ATLAS

English	Symbol	German
Motorway · Toll	Trento	Autobahn · Gebührenpflichtige
junction · Toll station ·		Anschlussstelle · Gebührenstelle ·
Junction with number ·		Anschlussstelle mit Nummer ·
Motel · Restaurant · Snackbar ·		Rasthaus mit Übernachtung ·
Filling-station ·		Raststätte · Kleinraststätte ·
Parking place with and without WC		Tankstelle · Parkplatz mit und ohne WC
Motorway under construction and	Datum Date	Autobahn in Bau und geplant mit
projected with completion date		Datum der Verkehrsübergabe
Dual carriageway (4 lanes)		Zweibahnige Straße (4-spurig)
Trunk road ·		Fernverkehrsstraße ·
Road numbers	14 E45	Straßennummern
Important main road		Wichtige Hauptstraße
Main road · Tunnel · Bridge		Hauptstraße · Tunnel · Brücke
Minor roads		Nebenstraßen
Track · Footpath		Fahrweg · Fußweg
Tourist footpath (selection)		Wanderweg (Auswahl)
Main line railway		Eisenbahn mit Fernverkehr
Rack-railway, funicular		Zahnradbahn, Standseilbahn
Aerial cableway · Chair-lift		Kabinenschwebebahn · Sessellift
Car ferry		Autofähre
Passenger ferry		Personenfähre
Shipping route		Schifffahrtslinie

English	Symbol	German
Nature reserve · Prohibited area		Naturschutzgebiet · Sperrgebiet
National park, natural park · Forest		Nationalpark, Naturpark · Wald
Road closed to motor vehicles	X X X X X	Straße für Kfz. gesperrt
Toll road		Straße mit Gebühr
Road closed in winter	XII-II	Straße mit Wintersperre
Road closed or not recommended for caravans		Straße für Wohnanhänger gesperrt bzw. nicht empfehlenswert
Tourist route · Pass	Weinstraße 1510	Touristenstraße · Pass
Scenic view · Panoramic view · Route with beautiful scenery		Schöner Ausblick · Rundblick · Landschaftlich bes. schöne Strecke

English	Symbol	German
Spa · Swimming pool		Heilbad · Schwimmbad
Youth hostel · Camping site		Jugendherberge · Campingplatz
Golf-course · Ski jump		Golfplatz · Sprungschanze
Church · Chapel		Kirche im Ort, freistehend · Kapelle
Monastery · Monastery ruin		Kloster · Klosterruine
Palace, castle · Ruin		Schloss, Burg · Schloss-, Burgruine
Tower · Radio-, TV-tower		Turm · Funk-, Fernsehturm
Lighthouse · Power station		Leuchtturm · Kraftwerk
Waterfall · Lock		Wasserfall · Schleuse
Important building · Market place, area		Bauwerk · Marktplatz, Areal
Arch. excavation, ruins · Mine		Ausgrabungs- u. Ruinenstätte · Bergwerk
Dolmen · Menhir · Nuraghe		Dolmen · Menhir · Nuraghen
Cairn · Military cemetery		Hünen-, Hügelgrab · Soldatenfriedhof
Hotel, inn, refuge · Cave		Hotel, Gasthaus, Berghütte · Höhle

Culture / Kultur

English		German
Picturesque town · Elevation	WIEN (171)	Malerisches Ortsbild · Ortshöhe
Worth a journey	★★ MILANO	Eine Reise wert
Worth a detour	★ TEMPLIN	Lohnt einen Umweg
Worth seeing	Andermatt	Sehenswert

Landscape / Landschaft

English		German
Worth a journey	★★ Las Cañadas	Eine Reise wert
Worth a detour	★ Texel	Lohnt einen Umweg
Worth seeing	Dikti	Sehenswert

Trips & Tours   **Ausflüge & Touren**

INDEX

This index lists all sights, museums and places, plus the names of important people featured in this guide. Numbers in bold indicate a main entry.

WRITE TO US

e-mail: info@marcopologuides.co.uk

Did you have a great holiday?
Is there something on your mind?
Whatever it is, let us know!
Whether you want to praise, alert us to errors or give us a personal tip – MARCO POLO would be pleased to hear from you.
We do everything we can to provide the very latest information for your trip.

Nevertheless, despite all of our authors' thorough research, errors can creep in. MARCO POLO does not accept any liability for this. Please contact us by e-mail or post.

MARCO POLO Travel Publishing Ltd
Pinewood, Chineham Business Park
Crockford Lane, Chineham
Basingstoke, Hampshire RG24 8AL
United Kingdom

PICTURE CREDITS

Cover photograph: Fishing boats in Kassiópi harbour (gettyimages/Robert Harding World Imagery: Rooney)
K. Bötig (1 bottom, 23, 53, 61, 87, 108); C. Dehnicke (3 top, 68/69, 93); DuMont Bildarchiv: Fabig (cover right, 98, 106, 112 top); Etrusco Restaurant (17 top); © fotolia.com: StrangerView (17 bottom); gettyimages/Robert Harding World Imagery: Rooney (1); Grecotel S.A. (84/85); R. Hackenberg (8, 20, 34, 36, 39, 54, 67, 108/109, 109); Huber: Dutton (26 left, 26 right); Huber: Giovanni Simeone (2 centre bottom, 10/11, 12/13, 18/19, 32/33, 62/63), Hanna Simeone (74), Johanna Huber (4), Mehlig (2 bottom, 48/49); F. Ihlow (3 bottom, 29, 30 left, 42, 47, 59, 94/95, 112 bottom, 113, 124/125); © iStockphoto.com: Alan Crawford (16 bottom), David H. Lewis (16 top), Ladida (16 centre); Laif/Hemis: Gardel (9); Laif: Hilger (57), IML (97), Kristensen (27, 79), Trummer (64); E. Laue (50, 60, 82); Look: Frei (28), Kreder (6); mauritius images: AGE (99), Axiom Photographic (103); Okapia: Kraus (72); T. Stankiewicz (cover left, 2 top, 3 centre, 5, 15, 24/25, 45, 78, 80/81, 89); Transit Archiv: Eisler (2 centre top, 7, 30 r., 37, 41, 96); vario images: Profimedia (91, 100/101), Westend61 (104/105); H. Wagner (70, 76/77)

1st Edition 2012

Worldwide Distribution: Marco Polo Travel Publishing Ltd, Pinewood, Chineham Business Park, Crockford Lane, Basingstoke, Hampshire RG24 8AL, United Kingdom. Email: sales@marcopolouk.com
© MAIRDUMONT GmbH & Co. KG, Ostfildern
Chief editors: Michaela Lienemann (concept, managing editor), Marion Zorn (concept, text editor)
Author: Klaus Bötig; Editor: Marlis von Hessert-Fraatz
Programme supervision: Ann-Katrin Kutzner, Nikolai Michaelis, Silwen Randebrock
Picture editor: Gabriele Forst
What's hot: wunder media, Munich
Cartography road atlas: © MAIRDUMONT, Ostfildern
Cartography pull-out map: © MAIRDUMONT, Ostfildern
Design: milchhof : atelier, Berlin;
Front cover, pull-out map cover, page 1: factor product munich
Translated from German by Robert McInnes; editor of the English edition: Christopher Wynne
Phrase book in cooperation with Ernst Klett Sprachen GmbH, Stuttgart, Editorial by Pons Wörterbücher

DOS & DON'TS

A few things you should bear in mind on Corfu

DON'T SHOW TOO MUCH SKIN

The Greeks have become used to naked skin in beach resorts. But further inland, many holidaymakers make fools of themselves by wearing too little. Your knees and shoulders must be covered in churches and monasteries.

DON'T ACT LIKE THE PAPARAZZI

Many Greeks like to be photographed but hate those holidaymakers who carry on as if they were on a photo safari. Before you release the shutter, smile at the person you want to photograph and wait for his or her agreement.

DON'T UNDERESTIMATE THE DANGER OF FIRE

The risk of a forest fire on Corfu is high. Smokers should be especially careful.

DON'T BE BROWBEATEN

Travel reps live from commissions. Most give honest information – but there are some black sheep who try to make their guests feel uncertain so that they will book their cars through them or take part in organised excursions instead of travelling by bus or taxi. Corfu is a safe island and there is no reason to be afraid of the locals.

DON'T ASK ABOUT THE COMPETITION

Greeks are fairly honest. But, if you go into a taverna and ask about another one – you will be told that it doesn't exist, that the innkeeper has died or the police have closed it down.

DON'T FORGET YOUR HIKING SHOES

Sandals are not even suitable for small hikes; you should at least wear sturdy trainers. The paths are often stony and slippery. And there are snakes – only a few and they are timid but you never know. Long trousers will protect you from thorns.

DON'T LEAVE TARMACED ROADS

If you leave the main road in your hire car, you will be driving without insurance and will have to pay for any damage. On Corfu, damage to the underside and tyres of the car is never covered by insurance!

DON'T BE SHOCKED BY THE PRICE OF FISH

Fresh fish has been extremely expensive in some Greek restaurants and tavernas for years. It is often sold by weight. You should ask how much a kilogram costs and be there when it is weighed so that you do not have any unpleasant surprises.